THE PROPHETIC ROMANCE

Fuchsia Pickett

CREATION
HOUSE

THE PROPHETIC ROMANCE by Fuchsia Pickett
Published by Creation House
A part of Strang Communications Company
600 Rinehart Road
Lake Mary, FL 32746
www.creationhouse.com

Unless otherwise noted, all Scripture quotations
are from the King James Version of the Bible.

Scripture quotations marked NAS are from the
New American Standard Bible. Copyright © 1960,
1962, 1963, 1968, 1971, 1972, 1973, 1975, 1977 by
the Lockman Foundation. Used by permission.

Library of Congress Catalog Card Number: 95-072168
ISBN: 0-88419-423-X

0 1 2 3 4 5 BBG 10 9 8 7 6 5
Printed in the United States of America

*To Dr. E. Judson Cornwall
my pastor of the faith,
colleague in ministry
and beloved spiritual brother.*

*I did not expect to become an author. It was
when I prepared two articles on the book of
Ruth for our church's monthly publication that
Dr. Judson Cornwall surprised me by making a
booklet of those articles and presenting them to
our annual ministers' conference. Through his
brotherly influence, I was inspired to put into
print the revelatory truths God had given me
to strengthen and bless the body of Christ.*

Contents

1

"HIStory" of Redemption

Tucked away among the massive history books of the Old Testament is the little book of Ruth, one of the most beautiful, historical love stories of all time. Its authentic historical account of a Jewish family's life rightfully places it with the history books in the canon of Scripture. However, after careful study we must conclude that the book of Ruth is more than an interesting and inspired book of history. It is "*HIS*tory" — the story of Christ — for Christ

Himself is clearly foreshadowed in this little book.

History Redefined

In the broadest sense, all of history can be characterized as *HIS*tory. We can evaluate all events of the human race, tragic as well as celebrated, on the basis of whether Christ, the revelation of God to man, was accepted or rejected. In this sense history may be defined as the study of mankind whom God made for the purpose of fellowshipping with Himself.

In this eternal perspective, even the rise and fall of nations throughout history becomes incidental to the great plan of God to redeem mankind. Though other definitions of history are valid, they are limited to man's temporal, finite parameters of understanding. History is more broadly defined according to the eternal purposes of God for mankind that can only be realized in Christ.

The Bible is the greatest history book ever written. It candidly describes mankind's dilemma of separation from God after fellowship was broken through man's disobedience. As well, it reveals the solution to that dilemma to be found through man's relationship to Christ. God's great plan to redeem mankind back to Himself through Christ's ultimate sacrifice of obedience is clearly outlined. All the Scriptures should be studied in this light, expecting to see Christ on every page revealed to us in His lovely character.

In Old Testament scriptural accounts, we see Christ prophetically in type, foreshadowed in the life of a biblical character or other historical reality. In the Gospels, we behold Him as He is, the Son of God in His personal dealings with the sons of men. Later, in the Epistles and other New Testament books, we see Him as the head of His church, established through the first apostles who recorded their story for us by the inspiration of the Holy Spirit. In the Revelation of John, we get a glimpse of the glorious future of mankind as Christ comes to reign as King of kings. So the history, as well as the future, of mankind is to be understood through revelation of Jesus Christ as He is seen throughout all Scripture.

The Church Foreshadowed

The little book of Ruth reveals eternal truths that foreshadow the revelation of the church — the body of Christ — that God was planning to bring to life hundreds of years later. As we watch the redemption of Ruth unfold, bringing her into relationship with her earthly bridegroom, we understand the divinely ordained "processes" the body of Christ must experience in order to come into relationship with her heavenly Bridegroom, Jesus Christ.

The concept of a woman foreshadowing the church is not strange to students of the Bible. In the New Testament, the church is referred to in the feminine gender. The Greek word for church, *ekklesia,* meaning "called out ones," carries a feminine ending. The church is also referred to in Scripture as the bride of Christ, a description of the love relationship we are to enjoy with Him. Men should have no more problem with being a part of the "bride of Christ" than we ladies have considering ourselves to be "sons of God." Both of these relationships with God pertain to male and female genders of mankind. They are language pictures that God uses to help us understand relationships that are eternal, not temporal in nature.

Understanding a Type

An understanding of typology in Scripture will unlock many of the deeper truths it teaches. As I explained in *For Such a Time as This,* my book on Esther:

> A careful foundation must be laid for the understanding of type and allegory so that we do not violate the true meaning of the Scriptures. A *type* is a person, thing or event that represents another, especially another that is to come in the future. Typology, the study of types, can bring to light many precious truths in the Word of God that are otherwise hidden to us. We can discover these truths as silver is discovered: by descending into a dark mine shaft and digging for them. An *allegory* is a story in which people, things and happenings have not only a literal significance, but a symbolic significance that is often morally instructive as well.

When Jesus taught about the shepherd who searched for his lost sheep, He was not telling the story of a specific event that happened in Galilee. He was using that natural illustration of a shepherd's care for his sheep to show the Father's love and care for each of His children. David portrayed the Lord as a shepherd in the poetic psalm that has spoken comfort to us throughout the centuries. How beautifully these word pictures help to reveal the nature of God to us! In the Old Testament, when animal sacrifices were initiated to atone for men's sins, God was foreshadowing prophetically the sacrifice of His Son at Calvary, the one death that would accomplish the reality of atonement. Those sacrifices were a type of the reality of Jesus' sacrifice to come.

There are three main types, or "skeletons," that walk through the book and unlock its truth from Genesis to Revelation. Following these pictures through the Bible provides a beautiful understanding of God's plan for His church. The first of these types is the picture of the tabernacle or temple. David's tabernacle and Solomon's temple reveal to us beautiful aspects of the worship that God desires. The Lord is intent on creating a temple of worship to bring into His presence. Paul admonishes believers, "Know ye not that ye are the temple of God?" (1 Cor. 3:16).

10

As New Testament Christians, each of us has become a habitation for the Spirit of God, a temple of worship where the King is to be enthroned.

A second type that unlocks the book is the picture of the human body or anatomy. The Bible depicts Christians as the body of Christ in the earth. Paul exhorts the Corinthians that they are "members in particular" of the body of Christ, and that God has set everyone in the body as it has pleased Him (1 Cor. 12:18,27).

The analogy of the bride and bridegroom is a third type that unlocks eternal truths throughout Scripture. Rebekah, Ruth and Esther give us beautiful insight into our relationship to Jesus Christ. God is preparing a bride for His Son to bring to the wedding feast of the Lamb.

So God communicates infinite, eternal truths through "picture language." We learn to look beyond the natural elements of truth in Scripture to receive the deeper allegorical truths they teach. The temple, the body of Christ and the bride of Christ are pictures that can be used like road maps to lead us ultimately to revelation of our heavenly Father, unfolding truth concerning Himself and His purposes for mankind. We can read the Bible for its literal history of recorded events or from a philosophical standpoint.

Not opening our minds, however, to parables, parabolic expressions, similes, metaphors, types and allegories will cause us to miss much of the understanding of what God is saying in His Word.

To properly understand type and allegory, we must realize that it is important not to attempt to make every word in a story fit a divine truth. There will usually be one or two spiritual truths to uncover from the otherwise natural event. We must be careful not to try to find types in every intricate detail of an allegory that was written to reveal a few major truths. No earthly story completely symbolizes an eternal truth. For example, Abraham represents God the Father in Scripture. Yet we see that Abraham sometimes did not act like God. Because of his humanity, he could not be a perfect type of the heavenly Father. Joseph is perhaps the most complete type of Christ in the Bible. There are over three hundred comparisons between his life and the life of Christ, but he was not a perfect man. These men did live out certain truths, however, in their natural lives that help us receive a spiritual message from a spiritual country and King.

We also must make sure that the truth revealed in the type can go through the cross. That is to say, the truth it teaches must relate without question to God's eternal plan for the salvation of mankind that was fulfilled through the shedding of Jesus' blood on Calvary. Each truth that is concealed in a type in the Old Testament is revealed in the New Testament reality of Jesus' sacrifice for the sin of mankind. Only as types and allegories help us to apply truth to our lives, and as they agree with all other Scripture, are they valid revelation. The ultimate purpose for all revelation must be to transform us into the image of Christ.[1]

A Love Story

Most of us have undoubtedly read and enjoyed the book of Ruth for its wonderful, historical love story. That is how I read it when I was a girl. For a high school literature course, I wrote an essay about the book of Ruth called "The Greatest Love Story." But I have since learned that the book of Ruth is much more than that. As we focus our attention on the allegorical meaning, we will marvel at the wonderful prophetic truths that are hidden in this romance.

In type, we are beholding the beautiful relationship of the church, the bride of Christ, to the Lord Jesus Christ, our heavenly Boaz. By understanding this divine love story, foreshadowed in the historical narrative, our lives can be changed for eternity.

New Beginnings

The book of Ruth is the eighth book in the Bible. In the study of numerology, numbers play a significant role in revealing the plan of redemption. The number eight in the Scriptures represents new beginnings. For example, the Scriptures record Noah's dramatic new beginning, saying that he was the eighth person saved in the flood (2 Pet. 2:5). In the New Testament, Christ taught eight beatitudes in the Sermon on the Mount (Matt. 5:1-9). These formed the basis of the constitution of the kingdom, the laws that would govern God's kingdom of love, and marked a new beginning for mankind. And Christ arose from the dead in resurrection power on the first day of the week, the eighth day, giving mankind their greatest new beginning.

As the eighth book of the Bible, Ruth is set in the canon as the book of new beginnings, revealing from earliest history God's desire to give a new beginning to those who would choose to follow Him.

The Canon of Scripture

In the study of the Scriptures we must be careful not to make a single verse stand on its own without relating to its context and relationship to other Scriptures. Similarly, the books themselves are related to the whole in their placement in the canon. A brief summary of the canon of Scripture surrounding Ruth will increase our appreciation for the wonderful revelation contained in this little book.

Genesis — The book of beginnings

In Genesis we witness the beginning of the universe, the beginning of man, the beginning of sin and the beginning of judgment. We also see the first glimpse of the hope of redemption, the promise of the coming Messiah (Gen. 3:16). Genesis also records for us the beginnings of the Hebrew race from Abraham, the Israelite race from Jacob and the Jewish race from Judah. Many other examples of "beginnings" can be found in the book of Genesis.

Exodus — The book of redemption

By the time in history of the book of Exodus, fallen man, who had continued to sin sorely against his God, desperately needed a redeemer. In the Exodus we see God's power of redemption through terrible plagues, through the blood of the Passover and through faith, delivering the children of Israel out of Egypt. Later, we witness the giving of the Law, which was redemption by discipline. The book of Exodus reveals to us much of God's purpose for the redemption of mankind.

Leviticus — The book of worship

Contrary to what some charismatic Christians may think, worship is not an expression of believers today that was "discovered" during the recent charismatic renewal. Worship was established by

God early in the history of mankind as the proper heart response to His wonderful redemption. God Himself shed the first blood sacrifice to clothe Adam and Eve's nakedness after their fall. Following that example, in the first recorded worship service in history, Abel offered an acceptable sacrifice of worship to the Lord, the firstlings of his flock, while Cain did not. The subsequent murder of Abel by his brother Cain revealed the wrong heart response that motivated Cain's sacrifice.

God's plan for worship was recorded many years later in the book of Leviticus. He established the priesthood of Aaron and his sons to help fulfill man's responsibility to worship the living God. The book of Leviticus describes an intricate system of sacrifices, feasts and oblations in the tabernacle of Moses that required a true heart response in the worship of God.

Whatever the external form, the essence of worship will always be man's heart response of love and gratitude to his Creator and Savior.

Numbers — The book of warfare

The book of warfare follows the book of worship. Warfare is an inevitable part of our walk with God. We must defeat our enemies to walk in victory and enjoy the promises of God. We can see a progression of our Christian walk by simply considering the order of the canon. From the fallen state of our beginning in Genesis, we behold our redemption in Exodus. That experience evokes the worship of Leviticus. Then, as seen in the book of Numbers, we must choose to come to maturity in our walk of faith through warfare, to "fight the good fight of faith" (1 Tim. 6:12). There is a promised land to be possessed, and as we witness the children of Israel gaining victory over their enemies, we understand that we have enemies to defeat — the world, the flesh and the devil — in order to gain our inheritance.

Deuteronomy — The book of obedience

Deuteronomy follows as a book of remembrance of God's mercy and grace as we obey Him. It reminds us that God requires our obedience to His laws in order to walk in fellowship with Him. It was Christ's perfect obedience to His Father that ultimately secured our redemption, requiring the awful sacrifice of His life on Calvary. In the New Testament, that obedient spirit is reflected in the words of Mary, the mother of our Lord, when she declared at the wedding that day, "Whatsoever he saith unto you, do it" (John 2:5). God desires our obedience above sacrifice of any kind.

We do not have to walk in legalism or sheer discipline to fulfill our obedience. We have been given the grace of God that creates in us the *desire* to obey Him. Three keys unlock God's kingdom: *surrender, faith* and *obedience.* Yielding to His will through surrender, having faith in what He said and walking in obedience to His will assures us of ultimate victory over all our enemies.

Joshua — The book of possessions

This historical book shows us how we can possess our inheritance by leaving the wilderness behind to cross over the Jordan and enter Canaan, our promised land. The waters of the Jordan river typify the death and burial of our sin and self-life. Through obedient warfare against our enemies we will conquer the promised land and enjoy the life of victory that God ordained for us from the beginning. God promised the Israelites that they could claim as their possession wherever they placed the soles of their feet. It was His responsibility to give the instructions for each battle. The children of Israel had only to obey those divine instructions to win the victory over their enemies.

Judges — The book of failure

Sadly, however, the conquering victories revealed in the book of Joshua were followed by the disobedience of the people we see recorded in the book of Judges. Israel had conquered much of Canaan; the people were possessing their inheritance. But they began to fail because of their disobedience and unbelief. They were not looking to God for direction as they once had. Judges 17:6 is a dismal commentary on that day: "In those days there was no king in Israel, but every man did that which was right in his own eyes." Periodically, God would judge the people's disobedience by allowing their enemies to rule over them. After a season of oppression they would cry unto Him and He would raise up deliverers for them.

Often this has been the commentary of the church and of our individual lives. During a period of personal disobedience, we have done what was right in our own eyes and have come under the oppression of our enemies. As a result, our lives are filled with fear and defeat. Then, God in His mercy delivers us and we enjoy a season of victory, only to find ourselves in bondage to yet another enemy of our souls after a time.

If that is the disappointing pattern of your Christian life, ask God for a new beginning — one that will bring you into complete abandonment to the will and purposes of God.

Ruth — The book of redemption

The book of Ruth follows the book of Judges, occurring historically during the time of the judges. It is not coincidental that famine filled the land during this time of general disobedience and failure. God had withdrawn His blessing on the land. Yet in His mercy, God turned to His people again and blessed their land. Thus we witness God's great desire to give mankind, whom He loves with such great love, a new beginning. He longs to bring restoration to the lives of those who will believe Him and follow Him. Most Bible scholars attribute the authorship of the book of Ruth to Samuel, the prophet, who also authored the books that bear his name.

First and Second Samuel — The books of the kingdom

The books of First and Second Samuel are significant in their placement in the canon as well. They set forth the royal kingdom established for the people of God, first under Saul and then David. These books teach many lessons regarding our walk and warfare.

For example, we dare not find ourselves in the place of Saul, who, after disobeying God to such a degree that the kingdom was taken from him, attempted to kill God's anointed man, David. David gives us a wonderful example of a man after God's own heart. Yet who among us has not cried with him, "Create in me a clean heart, O God; and renew a right spirit within me" (Ps. 51:10)? We should seek to emulate the godly qualities of these historical giants, and purpose to avoid their failures as we seek to establish the kingdom of God on earth.

The little book of Ruth does not compare in size to these massive volumes of history to which it is related by its placement in the canon. Yet, the truths it contains are just as powerful for us to understand. It reveals eternal principles of redemption that thrill our hearts and help us pursue the kingdom. And it foreshadows the dealings of God with His church — His bride — in a most beautiful way.

The Little Books

The little books of the Bible should not seem

insignificant because of their smallness. Their value is not diminished because of their size. For example, the brevity of Obadiah's challenging vision does not diminish the power of the divine truth it reveals.

The book of Esther, another little book, beautifully foreshadows the personal relationship of the true worshiper with God. It portrays the miraculous deliverance of the bride of Christ from her enemies equally as well as the book of Ruth, though set in a completely different historical and economical background. What profound drama and prophetic insight we would miss if the canon had not included the little book of Esther! I explore the richness of Esther in my book, *For Such a Time as This*.[2]

In the New Testament, the book of Philemon is a beautiful picture of redemption. Paul's poignant entreaty for a runaway slave to be restored, not to his former state as a slave, but as a beloved brother, helps us understand God's compassion toward those bound to sin. Through redemption, we are no longer slaves, but members of the family of God; loved, accepted and free from the debt of our sin. What priceless revelation of the love of God is found in these twenty-five verses of Scripture.

If the little book of Jude had not been placed into the canon of Scripture, we would never have known that Enoch was a prophet (v. 14). Nor would we have been given the understanding of the seven awful steps to apostasy (vv. 5,6,8,10,11) or known that Satan wrestled for the body of Moses (v. 9). And we would not have been given the comforting promise, "Now unto him that is able to keep you from falling, and to present you faultless before the presence of his glory with exceeding joy, to the only wise God our Saviour, be glory and majesty, dominion and power, both now and ever. Amen" (vv. 24-25).

We conclude then, that the truths revealed by the smaller books of the canon are as powerful as the longest narratives. The book of Ruth is one of those powerful little books that reveals to us allegorically what is involved in our own personal redemption as well as that of the body of Christ corporately. Not only Ruth's circumstances, but her attitudes, desires and decisions relating to those circumstances, speak eternal truths on which the restoration of all the blessings of God for our lives depend. Other characters in the narrative teach us by example as well, mirroring the consequences of our own choices and attitudes and helping us evaluate our relationships with God.☙

2

Titles — Significant in Redemption's Plan

When the Lord began to open my eyes to the allegorical truths of the book of Ruth, a simple outline of words beginning with the letter *t* emerged. The first *t* of the outline involves the significance of titles. In ancient cultures, titles and names carried much greater significance than they do in most of our modern cultures.

Old Testament names often revealed one's character prophetically. For example, Jacob's name means "supplanter and cheater." Those qualities characterized his life as he sought to take the blessing of God from his brother, Esau. In some instances, names were given to mark an event in history. When the glory of God departed from the house of Israel while the wife of the priest was giving birth, she named her son Ichabod, which means "the glory is departed" (1 Sam. 4:21).

Names were changed for specific reasons, especially when one had an encounter with God. When God established the covenant with Abram, He changed Abram's name to Abraham, adding the h with the rough breathing sound ha that represents the breath of God. In the New Testament, Jesus called Simon to be His disciple. Simon means "reed," and carries the connotation of weakness and instability. Jesus changed Simon's name to Peter, which means "rock," signifying prophetically the strength of character this apostle would one day demonstrate in the kingdom of God. Many other examples could be given of Bible characters whose names were changed as a result of the redeeming power of God touching their lives.

Names of God

God reveals Himself to us in the Scriptures in three ways: through His names, through His acts and through His descriptions of Himself. There are over 350 names of God in the Bible. Each one reveals a wonderful aspect of His nature. For example, when Abraham went to the mount to sacrifice his son, Isaac, he discovered God as *Jehovah-Jireh,* the "One who provides." When we are born again, we come to know God as our *Redeemer.* Then, as our relationship with Him matures, we discover Him to be our *Wisdom,* our *Peace* and the *Lord of Hosts.* When walking through sorrow and difficulty, we are relieved to learn that He is our faithful *Shepherd* and *Guide.* Every new revelation of Himself through His names enlarges our capacity to know Him.

God also reveals Himself through His acts. We learn what the power of God is like as we read of God dividing the waters, raising the dead and stilling the storms. His powerful judgments against the cities of Sodom and Gomorrah show how God feels about evil.

Jesus was the express image of the Father, accurately revealing God in everything He did. His descriptions of Himself also show us the Father. Jesus said of Himself, "I am the way, the truth, and the life" (John 14:6). He called Himself the "good shepherd."

It is customary in our culture to give a person one or two names. We could never expect to describe God in one or two names. If all of heaven could not contain God, one name could never explain Him. Yet as we cultivate our relationship with Him, His names reveal the loveliness of His person. Through His names, through His acts and by His descriptions of Himself, God has continually sought to reveal who He is to mankind.

The Characters

If I remember my study of rhetoric correctly, the five essential parts to a story are: an introduction, the characters, a plot, a main point of interest and a conclusion. My heavenly Father knew about literature long before any English teacher ever did. The book of Ruth is a well-written, divinely-inspired story. It is an accurate historical account of events that really happened in people's lives. It is also an allegory of things to come.

The biblical names of places and characters in the book of Ruth are filled with prophetic revelation. We will miss much of the significance of the story from God's viewpoint if we do not understand the names. Reading Ruth from an earthly viewpoint gives us factual historical information. Reading it from God's perspective helps us understand the heavenly truths God wants to communicate to us.

The setting for the book of Ruth is the town of Bethlehem-judah. *Bethlehem* means "house of bread." *Judah* signifies "a place where people praise God." The name *Bethlehem-judah* characterizes life as a place of bountiful provision and joy. Unfortunately, we observe from the narrative that the people in Bethlehem-judah are presently suffering from famine. We will discuss the reasons for that sad fact in a later chapter.

As the book opens, we are introduced to the family of Elimelech living in the land of Bethlehem-judah. *Elimelech* means "God is King." He represents a godly man, rearing his children in the place of provision and praise. His wife's name is Naomi, which means "pleasant." Her presence in the home filled it with pleasantness for her husband and her two sons to enjoy as she nurtured her family in the place of praise.

Elimelech and Naomi named their first son *Mahlon,* which means "joy." They called their second son *Chilion,* meaning "song." These boys were the fruit of two lives lived in the presence of God's provision. Speaking allegorically, what a lovely home it would be where God is King, pleasantness fills the home, the song of the Lord is heard and the joy of the Lord is their strength. This happy family is a testimony of the complete provision believers have in Christ. This blessed family is a type of our Christian walk as God intends it to be.

As the redeemed church today, God intends for our lives to be characterized as a house of bread and a place of praise. According to the Scriptures, every believer is a temple of the Holy Spirit. For our temples to become a Bethlehem-judah, we must learn to feed on God's Word, allowing it to transform our character. As we learn to cultivate Christ's presence in our lives, His pleasantness will fill our hearts individually. Then we can respond corporately, as the church, filled with a song of joy as we come to God's house to worship together.

Ruth, for whom the book is named, is the central figure of the narrative. She is actually one of three main characters in the story. Naomi has equal importance to the story. She played a redemptive role in the life of Ruth and foreshadows other important prophetic truths.

The meaning of Naomi's name "pleasant" carries allegorical significance as it relates to the Scriptures. The Scriptures teach that the knowledge of God is pleasant. The writer of the Proverbs declared, "When wisdom entereth into thine heart, and knowledge is pleasant unto thy soul; Discretion shall preserve thee, understanding shall keep thee" (Prov. 2:10-11). Again, he declared that the ways of wisdom "are ways of pleasantness, and all her paths are peace" (Prov. 3:17).

Filling our hearts with the wisdom of God will not guarantee that all our circumstances will be pleasant. But inside the sanctuary of our hearts we can experience joy and peace even in difficult situations because the Word of God abides there. God's provision is abundant when we walk in yielded obedience to His ways. He never intended us to suffer famine in our personal lives or in our churches. The church is to be characterized as a house of bread, filled with the living Word.

Naomi is a type of the present church age. The famine she experienced reflects the terrible spiritual famine of the presence of God that much of the church has experienced for many years. Yet as early as the time of this eighth book of the Old Testament, we see foreshadowed God's wonderful plan for restoration of His church.

As we identify with Naomi's desperate situation in the opening of the story and walk with her to her journey's end, we will rejoice to see her nursing her grandson as a fruit of her restoration. Applying the allegory, we can look forward with great anticipation to having the presence of God restored to our lives personally and to the church corporately, especially as we see how God's heart yearns for restoration and initiates it as well.

Boaz, whom we meet later in the narrative, is the third main character. A wealthy lord of the land, Boaz demonstrates his integrity as the near kinsman-redeemer by his kindness and willingness to fulfill the law of redemption for Ruth. As a type of Christ, Boaz reveals the redemptive love of Christ, who willingly laid down His life that we might be redeemed. Redemptive love will always be recognized by its quality of self-sacrifice. Redemptive love alone can bring us to complete restoration.

The book of Ruth ranks among the greatest books of the Bible for teaching true, spiritual restoration, foreshadowed in the redemptive love of Boaz for Ruth. Though we can learn important lessons from others in the narrative, it is these three — Naomi, Ruth and Boaz — upon whom we will focus our attention.

Because of the famine in Bethlehem-judah, Elimelech decided to take his family to Moab. In this Jewish family's plight, we witness the tragic loss that is a result of famine. We can apply the allegorical truths regarding famine to our personal lives as well as to our churches. The absence of God's presence as our sufficiency signals the presence of a spiritual famine. It is not pleasant to relate to the tragic loss of this family. But as we evaluate our own "land of famine," we will experience the hope that arises as we witness the everlasting love and kindness of our Redeemer, bringing restoration to those who choose to be restored.🍂

3

Famine's Tragedy —
A Cry for Redemption

The land of Moab was filled with idolatry. The Moabites, enemies of Israel for many years, were not allowed to enter the land of Israel. Allegorically, Moab is a type of the carnal life, the self-life of the believer. It represents a Christian who is still ruled by a carnal mind, making decisions without the benefit of the bread of the living Word. Moab is a land where God does not reign as King and where we are exposed to idols of many kinds. The most

31

obvious idol worshiped there is self.

As born-again believers, we have been delivered from Egypt, a type of our sinful life before salvation. But we must also be delivered from "Moab," a type of our carnal nature, in order to come to spiritual maturity in Christ. The apostle Paul declares, "to be carnally minded is death; but to be spiritually minded is life and peace. Because the carnal mind is enmity against God: for it is not subject to the law of God, neither indeed can be" (Rom. 8:6-7). Elimelech did not take his family back to Egypt, but to Moab — a place of carnality that resulted in the terrible loss of the presence of God.

When Elimelech chose to leave Bethlehem-judah, he chose to expose himself and his family to a host of foreign gods and to a life of idolatry. It is significant that he eventually died in this place. The beginning of Naomi's tragedy is the second *t* in our alliterated outline. Elimelech's tragic death left Naomi to face life as a widow in this foreign land with her two sons. A widow's plight was never pleasant in those days. Unless it was possible for a near kinsman-redeemer to help her, she was usually reduced to begging. In this idolatrous land, the possibility of a kinsman-redeemer did not exist.

Allegorically, many believers find themselves living in an "idolatrous foreign land" because of the famine of the presence of God in their personal lives and in the church. In the land of Moab, Naomi no longer had God as her king and had lost her joy and song. Contrast this sorrow with the fact that she had once lived in the house of bread, in the presence of God. Is that not the testimony of many Christians today who enjoyed the presence of God in their lives at one time but have lost their joy through circumstances of life?

Naomi's sons, Mahlon and Chilion, settled into life in Moab. They married Moabitish girls, strengthening their ties to the idolatrous land. But the two happy boys that left Bethlehem-judah, whose names mean "joy" and "song," did not have a bright future. Eventually, both died in the land of Moab, leaving a household of three widows struggling for survival.

The famine which had invaded the land of Bethlehem-judah spread throughout the surrounding countries. Naomi, who had fled with her family from the famine in Bethlehem-judah, now found herself in Moab, widowed, destitute and alone with her two widowed daughters-in-law.

The happy lifestyle Naomi and her family enjoyed in Bethlehem-judah had deteriorated to the devastating circumstances in Moab. As she faced the stark reality of her situation, Naomi must have cried out in desperation, "How could this have happened to me?"

Causes of Famine

How could famine invade Bethlehem-judah, a land characterized as the House of Bread and Place of Praise? How could natural laws of harvest be so affected that instead of producing the expected bounty of bread for its inhabitants, a fertile land was wasted by famine, violating the character of its name?

Relating to this question allegorically, perhaps even a more poignant question could follow: Can the church today experience a famine, the church that has been a reservoir for truth and revelation, a place of fresh bread to feed the hungry? Where believers have stood and worshiped God exuberantly? Where the song of the Lord has been heard? Could there come a famine to that land? Sadly, the one answer to these questions is yes. Today, much of Christendom finds itself tragically estranged from the presence of God, given to the idolatry of the land, having left the House of Bread because of famine. The question yet to be answered then is, How does famine come to the church? And perhaps more importantly, How can spiritual famine be averted?

1. Wrong Government

Judges were ruling the land of Bethlehem-judah when God withdrew His blessing, allowing famine to result. It was not in the divine order of God's plan of government to have judges rule the people. God had established a theocracy for His people and intended to rule as King Himself, speaking to His people through the prophets and priests. However, as disobedience caused the people of Israel to fall into bondage to their enemies again and again, judges were raised up to deliver them. The Scriptures declare that during this troubled time every man did what was right in his own eyes (Judg. 17:6). Without godly leadership, the people fell into idolatry, foreign political domination, intermarriage with pagans and lived in a general state of spiritual confusion. They had forsaken the living God.

Unfortunately, much of the church world today has forsaken the godly pattern of leadership that He established for His church. It was never God's intention that His church be governed by boards, committees and the "vote of the majority." God ordained that Christ should be the head of the church. As the head of His body, Christ gave to the church apostles, prophets, evangelists and pastor-teachers — often called the fivefold ministry — to direct the church under the leadership of the Holy Spirit (see Eph. 4). He has chosen to govern the church through the leadership of the Holy Spirit by those men and women that He has anointed and given as gifts to the church for leadership. If we choose to follow a method of church government other than that designed by God, we will experience a famine of the presence of God in our churches. The government of God must be restored to the church according to the biblical pattern in order for her to enjoy the blessing of God.

2. Idolatry

When we turn away from worship of the true and living God, we soon discover that we are worshiping at the altar of idols. Worship of the living God must be restored to its rightful place in our individual lives and in the church. For that to happen, we must allow the Holy Spirit to cleanse us from idolatry. Worship must become a reality in our lives, not simply an activity to take up time in a church service. God created mankind with an innate need to worship.

Our idols may not be made out of wood or stone and sitting in our houses, but they will be idols just the same — idols of our time, family, job, money, things or friends. Perhaps TV absorbs us and poisons our minds with the philosophy of humanism. If so, it has become our idol. Sports, recreation, even leisure times can become idols if we give them the wrong place in our lives. My friend, Dutch Sheets, defines idolatry clearly as, "Whatever becomes our ultimate concern is what we are worshiping."[1] We can expect to experience famine of the blessing of God if we turn from worshiping the living God, replacing Him with the worship of other idolatrous things. Worship is not optional in the House of Bread if we are to enjoy God's blessing.

3. Disobedience

Famine results when we continually transgress God's laws, knowing to do right and not doing it. Obedience to the laws of God brings wonderful blessings to our lives. The converse is also true — disobedience brings terrible consequences. The prophet Isaiah understood this dual reality when he declared, "If ye be willing and obedient, ye shall eat the good of the land: but if ye refuse and rebel, ye shall be devoured with the sword" (Is. 1:19-20). The relationship of cause and effect is clearly stated here: eating the good of the land depends on our willing obedience to the laws of God, while death comes through our rebellion and disobedience. We cannot expect to have the blessings of God on our lives if we walk in disobedience to His commands.

4. Lack of Repentance

A lack of repentance will bring famine to our souls. Repentance has been misunderstood by many in the church to be only the initial act of receiving salvation. Repentance is not a onetime act; it is a state of grace that we must allow to work in our hearts continually. True repentance is a cry that says, "I'm not satisfied with what I am. I thank God I am not who I was. But I am not yet who I am going to be. I repent of who I am and that I am not what I am supposed to be. With that repentant attitude I cry out, 'Change me, O God.'"

When I receive a revelation of the holiness of God as Isaiah did when he saw the seraphim crying out, "Holy, holy, holy is the Lord of hosts: the whole earth is full of his glory" (Is. 6:3), then I will cry with him, "Woe is me! for I am undone" (v. 5). In that place of worship, the Holy Spirit changes me, cleansing me with a coal taken from the altar of God (vv. 6-7). With each new revelation of the holiness of God, I receive revelation of my need for cleansing. If I do not experience the continual cleansing that comes through repentance, I will become a victim of famine in my soul.

The church will experience a deeper work of repentance in the coming revival than we have ever known. I'm not referring to an unhealthy melancholy introspection, but to a cry born by revelation of the Spirit of God to be changed into the image of Christ. As we worship the Lamb of God, beholding Him in all His purity and loveliness, we will see the contrast of our sinful state. That reality will cause us to cry out for cleansing by His blood. We will see our lack of love for the brethren, our prejudices, disunity, independence, self-seeking and idolatry. As we cry out for cleansing from these and other sins, He will cleanse us. We will become the glorious church without spot or wrinkle He has ordained for us to become — a worthy bride for our Lord Jesus Christ.

These are not all-inclusive causes of famine; there are others. Anything that keeps us from the presence of God for any length of time will bring famine to our individual lives and churches. Yet, God has clearly revealed the pathway to preserving His divine blessings on our lives. Establishing the divine government of God in the church, experiencing heartfelt worship, walking in obedience to His Word and living a life of repentance will water the soil of our hearts and keep them from becoming hard and unyielding. Our soft hearts will be able to receive the life-giving water of the Holy Spirit poured into them by prayer and through the Word of God. In this way we will prevent the terrible consequences of famine from coming to our lives and destroying our souls.

Hope for the Church

The church in America has experienced a long, dry spell. Studies show that many who have once considered themselves orthodox Christians have turned from the faith to become involved in Eastern religions and New Age philosophies and even Satanism as their practiced religion.[2] In spite of that current trend, however, we are also seeing positive changes in the climate of the American church.

God is beginning to visit His people again with a renewal and refreshing that is crossing denominational barriers. One example is what some have called the "laughing revival." God is giving to His church a divine refreshing that is restoring the joy of the Lord to thousands of Christians in America and other nations. Though this manifestation of God's presence alone does not constitute revival, I believe it reflects the beginning of a visitation of God that will culminate in a greater revival in the church than we have ever seen before.

In October 1963, the Holy Spirit gave me an indelible vision of the coming revival. He unveiled the years ahead and let me see what was going to happen in the last days in the church age. As I waited before Him in prayer for two days, He showed me the detailed construction of a divine hydroelectric power plant. He showed me how He was building a network of churches and running primary and secondary lines, digging out reservoirs and filling them with the water of His Word.

Finally, I saw Him put His hand on a great power switch and I heard Him say, "This time when I pull that great switch and release the rivers of My living Word in their fullness, no demon, devil, man or denomination will ever dam it up again. I will do a quick work; I am going to bring revival that will result in the ingathering of the great harvest of souls."[3] That vision was given to me over thirty years ago, and I have preached it as a coming reality everywhere I have traveled. Recently, during a conference at Shekinah Ministries in Blountville, Tennessee, I again saw the hand of God on that great power switch, ready to pull it to loose the waters of revival that will flood the earth. In God's time, when that happens, "the earth shall be filled with the knowledge of the glory of the Lord, as the waters cover the sea" (Hab. 2:14). Anyone can be a part of God's great revival who does not allow famine to rule in his or her soul.

As believers, we dare not live many days without allowing the moving of the Holy Spirit in our hearts. To do so is to guarantee the beginning of personal famine. Besides cultivating our relationships with God, we need to guard against holding offenses against our brothers and sisters. Offense grows the weeds of bitterness. We can't afford to be bitter. You may ask, "What if we have been hurt by people?" Who hasn't? Jesus is bigger than any hurt. We must choose to let Him rule in our hearts in love and forgiveness.

Holding offenses will grieve the Holy Spirit and hinder His work in our lives. When the Holy Spirit quits brooding over our spirits, it is not long until our prayer life seems dead. A dead prayer life is a symptom of famine in the land.

If our lives are not bathed in prayer, personal witnessing becomes a chore, joyous testimony ceases, our standard of consecration is lowered and we don't want to hear sermons on commitment. These are all signs of famine. Some people may even choose to go to Moab, where the Lord is no longer King of their lives and where their song dies, their joy is gone and their pleasantness turns to bitterness. If these symptoms of famine are present in our lives, we need to ask the Holy Spirit to give us true repentance and to fill our spirits with prayer.

Hope in Her Tragedy

God's great mercy and loving-kindness continually extends kindness to His erring children. In her desperate state, having lost everything of value that she had when she left Bethlehem-judah, Naomi heard that the Lord had visited His people there in giving them bread (Ruth 1:6). Hearing that good news brought hope to Naomi's heart, filling her with desire to return home. The third *t* in our outline involves Naomi's dramatic turning, bringing hope into the tragedy she has been living. True repentance involves a turn in the opposite direction. It was Naomi's turning that marked the beginning of her restoration.❦

4

The Turning of Naomi

*D*ecisions that require great changes in our lifestyles are never easy to make. Though Naomi may have longed many times to return to her homeland of Bethlehem-judah where she was raised, she had undoubtedly grown accustomed to life in Moab during the years she lived there. She had buried her loved ones in Moab and had become attached to her daughters-in-law as well. It would require a painful uprooting of her life once more in order to return to her homeland. Yet when she heard that God was visiting His people, her heart was stirred. It was this good news of God's visitation to His people that persuaded Naomi to return to the House of Bread.

> Then she arose with her daughters-in-law, that she might return from the country of Moab: for she had heard in the country of Moab how that the Lord had visited his people in giving them bread. Wherefore she went forth out of the place where she was, and her two daughters-in-law with her; and they went on the way to return unto the land of Judah (Ruth 1:6-7).

In one of Jesus' parables, hunger for fresh bread was the motivation for the return of the prodigal son to his father's house (Luke 15:17-20). The remembrance that even servants in his father's house had more than enough bread to eat brought this wayward boy to his senses and started him on his journey homeward to his father's house. Finding himself in a desperate state of famine, the prodigal's hunger reminded him of the fresh bread to be found in his father's house. Hope of receiving that bread caused him to turn from the wasteful life of a prodigal and return to the blessing of his father's house, where all was restored to him as a son.

Hunger, that state of need that refuses to be denied satisfaction, is a gift of God. It is this gift of hunger that serves to bring us to the place of

God's blessing. Jesus said, "Blessed are they which do hunger and thirst after righteousness: for they shall be filled" (Matt. 5:6). Spiritual hunger is wonderfully redemptive as we seek to satisfy it with God's provision. Naomi's life had become empty according to her own admission. She said, "I went out full, and the Lord hath brought me home again empty" (Ruth 1:21). She did not seem to understand that hunger or emptiness could be a blessing, but in deciding to return to the House of Bread, she had placed her life in the Lord's hands. Perhaps He would fill her once again.

The Disciplining Hand of God

Many times difficult situations serve to turn us to God in a way that brings unexpected blessing into our lives. Often we do not recognize the disciplining hand of God in our negative circumstances. In order to get Naomi out of the land of Moab, the place of carnal compromise, God had to lay His hand heavily upon her. She suffered the loss of her husband and sons who represented allegorically the presence of God in her life. When Naomi arrived home in Bethlehem-judah, she testified to those who met her that she had been under the disciplining hand of God: "I went out full, and the Lord hath brought me home again empty: why then call ye me Naomi, seeing the Lord hath testified against me, and the Almighty hath afflicted me?" (Ruth 1:21).

We might not be so candid as Naomi to say that God has afflicted us, but we can relate to bitter experiences that brought us to God in our searches for relief from our pain. Sometimes Christians have misunderstood their painful experiences, feeling that God was punishing them for displeasing Him. We must not consider painful times of chastening under the hand of God to be punishment. *Punishment,* as defined by Webster, is "suffering, pain, or loss that serves as retribution." There is a vast difference between discipline and punishment. God does not punish His children. God's wrath and punishment, which will be poured out during the great tribulation, is reserved for the devil and his angels. Jesus bore the wrath of God for our sins on Calvary. He bore our punishment, so that if we accept the sacrifice of Christ we will never have to know God's wrath. God will never pour out His wrath in judgment on His church. We do not serve an angry God who is waiting to punish His children when they do wrong.

There are times, however, when God becomes a good disciplinarian. Though His discipline may be painful to us, His motivation for correcting us is not to punish us, but to shape and mold us into His image. Often our response to His correction is to whine and cry as children do when parents correct them. What we fail to understand at those times, as children do as well, is that discipline, though painful, is a very important expression of love. It saves us from the evil tendencies that would ultimately destroy us if left unchecked in our lives.

Our Loving Father

It is important for parents to understand the difference between punishment and discipline. Parents should never punish their children in anger, expressing only their frustration with their child. Children should be lovingly and firmly disciplined for wrongdoing and then personally affirmed with expressed affection. That will let them know they are loved, but the behavior that brought the discipline was wrong and should not be repeated.

One of my most pleasant memories of the church I founded in Texas occurred when we had set aside three days for fasting and prayer as a congregation. The church was open during the day for people to come at mealtimes to pray, and each evening we met together for prayer. On the third evening of our corporate fast, I invited the congregation to share with each other something the Lord had shown them during these days or what He had done for them personally.

Many of the people stood, with softened hearts, to share a time of repentance or an understanding of the Scriptures that God had given them. Then Cliff, a red-headed, seven-year-old boy stood up and asked to share. He began to cry as he said, "Pastor, Jesus talked to me during these three days of fasting and prayer."

I asked, "Clifford, what did He tell you?"

Crying hard, the little boy struggled to speak. "He has been telling me to thank my daddy and mother for loving me enough to spank me." Then he sobbed out, "Daddy, I love you."

At Clifford's confession, the entire congregation wept in gratitude as they related to the loving discipline of our heavenly Father. Such discipline demonstrates a deeper revelation of the love of God in our lives.

Becoming Disciples

In the word *discipline,* we can readily see the word *disciple.* When God disciplines us, it is to make us true disciples of Christ. God disciplined Naomi in the land of Moab by allowing her song and joy, and the presence of her King, to be taken from her. He laid His hand heavily upon her until, in her desperate situation, she was willing to leave Moab and return empty to the House of Bread. Many times, that is what happens to us before we enter into the true blessing of God. There has to be a brokenness in our hearts that says, "Forgive me for not wanting to be corrected." God has promised to dwell with those who have a broken and contrite spirit (Is. 57:15). Brokenness, which is often a result of discipline, is a prerequisite for truly finding God.

God is not an adversary. He is not against us. He sometimes allows us to experience the pain of affliction for our good. The church today is being called to return to prayer and repentance. Our heavenly Father is putting His hand of discipline on the church and calling her to return home to His presence. That is what brings revival — a turning of hearts to God in deep contrition.

For many years I thought when I went through adversity that God was mad at me. I did not understand His loving discipline. But on the morning that I was carried into a Pentecostal church, close to death from a fatal disease, God spoke very clearly to my heart: "If ye be willing and obedient, ye shall eat the good of the land" (Is. 1:19). He asked me — a Methodist minister — if I would be willing to identify with those Pentecostal people.

I answered, "Yes, I will identify with them." In that service I was dramatically healed and received the baptism of the Holy Spirit.[1] God was asking me to turn from my theological background and doctrinal position and all that was "comfortable" to me in my knowledge of God. He asked me to go with Him to the House of Bread into fresh revelation of an almighty God. He tested my heart with the questions, "Daughter, will you turn? Will you let Me take you home where there is bread?" In my desperate physical condition, I found the grace to say, "Yes, Lord." When I returned to the doctors the next week, they examined me and declared me healed of that fatal disease.

That dramatic turning opened the Word of God to my heart through divine revelation by the Holy Spirit. I experienced, as Naomi eventually did, the divine restoration of a greater revelation and presence of God in my life than I had known before. That revelation of Himself has continually increased in the years that have followed as I have purposed to "eat" of His Word in the House of Bread.

I wish I could say that from the time of my

physical healing I have not suffered any other adversity. Though that is not the case. I have learned, even in adversity, that God's hand is never upon our lives in punishment. His chastening, though painful, is always intended to bring redemption. I understand more than ever how much my heavenly Father loves me. His discipline is simply an expression of His great love. Punishment belongs to the devil and his angels; chastisement belongs to the child of God for the purpose of bringing correction to his or her life. Naomi had yet to learn this wonderful truth of God's faithfulness in His chastening hand on her life.

The Time of the Barley Harvest

Naomi returned to Bethlehem-judah at the beginning of the barley harvest. According to historians, barley was one of the most important grains raised in Palestine. It was grown chiefly for animals but was also eaten by the poor. It was sown in the fall and harvested the following spring. In the lowlands, it was harvested in April. In the hill country, it was not harvested until May or the beginning of June. The wheat harvest came four weeks later.

Firstfruits were waved as an offering before the Lord during the barley harvest (Lev. 23:10). According to the Law, sheaves of barley were brought to the priest to be waved before the Lord as an offering of thanksgiving. These Old Testament offerings foreshadow beautiful truths for New Testament worship. The lifting of our hands in worship is that expression of praise foreshadowed by the Old Testament pattern of the wave offering. Speaking allegorically, Naomi's return during the firstfruits of barley harvest is being mirrored in the visitation of praise and worship the church has enjoyed during the last few years. Around the world, thousands of Christians from every denomination have experienced a fresh anointing on their corporate worship. They are offering the firstfruits of thanksgiving to the Lord, waving their hands and praising God.

Many Christians are learning to praise God in a new dimension, turning their feet back to the House of Bread and opening their hearts to the revival that is coming. A lengthy process of preparation remains before the church can enjoy her complete restoration. But that restoration would not be possible without the wave offering of praise experienced during this initial turning in the time of barley harvest — the harvest for the poor.

As we recognize our poverty of spirit, the words of Jesus will be fulfilled for us: "Blessed are the poor in spirit: for theirs is the kingdom of heaven" (Matt. 5:3). If Naomi had not acknowledged her poverty and turned from her life in the land of Moab, she would not have experienced even the beginning of redemption that the barley harvest represents.

Naomi could not effect her own restoration, a kinsman-redeemer would be required for that. But she had positioned herself for redemption by returning to the House of Bread. In that same way, though the church is powerless to restore the holiness, evangelistic zeal and manifest presence of God that she lost during the years of famine, she must choose to respond to the news of God's fresh visitation. For the church to be truly restored, she must turn, determining to position herself in the land where God is bringing fresh revelation of His Word and a demonstration of His mercies.❦

5

A Testing of Hearts

As is usually the case, Naomi's turning affected other lives besides her own. The lives of her daughters-in-law were intertwined with hers, and they were faced with decisions regarding their own futures because of Naomi's decision to return to the House of Bread. This testing of their hearts brings us to the fourth *t* in our outline. For Ruth and Orpah, going to the House of Bread meant leaving their homeland and kindred behind. It meant they would have to leave everything that was familiar to them, severing all family ties, to live as foreigners in the land of Bethlehem-judah.

Though both girls initially made the decision to go with their mother-in-law, it seems that Naomi did not want to take the responsibility for those decisions. Thanking them for their kindness to her, she plainly told them to stay in their mother's home. At the same time she was definitely testing their motivation. She declared that she could not provide husbands for them to secure their futures. Both girls wept, revealing the pain that Naomi's decision caused them. Yet, each responded differently.

Before they completed their journey to Bethlehem-judah, Orpah chose to return to her own homeland, content to live her life in a place of idolatry. Orpah chose to remain with the familiar, though it meant losing the touch of the presence of God she had seen in Naomi's life. But Ruth pleaded with Naomi to let her go with her to serve the living God. Ruth chose to accept the call, take the challenge and make the commitment to enter into covenant relationship with the God of Naomi.

> And Ruth said, Entreat me not to leave thee, or to return from following after thee: for whither thou goest, I will go; and where thou lodgest, I will lodge: thy people shall be my people, and thy God my God: Where thou diest, will I die, and there will I be buried: the Lord do so to me, and more also, if aught but death part thee and me (Ruth 1:16-17).

53

Choices of Destiny

The power of choice that God has given to every person cannot be underestimated. How dramatically our right to choose affects the course of our lives! Naomi's choice to return to Bethlehem-judah would ultimately result in her personal restoration. Ruth's choice to follow Naomi and to serve Naomi's God brought her to a wonderful destiny. Orpah's name means "stiff-necked or skull." The decision Orpah made to stay in Moab reflected the inflexible, unyielding character described by her name and resulted in her death in obscurity — she was never heard of again. Such is the end of stiff-necked people. It is better to have a harnessed heart than a stiff neck.

Ruth's name means "friend." She proved her friendship to Naomi and to God by her willingness to leave all she held dear to follow Naomi and serve her God. This beauty of character is to be revealed throughout the rest of the narrative as Ruth gains a reputation in the whole city of Bethlehem-judah as a virtuous woman. Ruth and Orpah's hearts were both tested by the same circumstances. The choices that each girl made in these circumstances dramatically affected the entire course of their lives.

No one can force us to go to the House of Bread. We choose to go. That power of choice — the decision of our wills — becomes the key factor in whether or not we possess what God has provided for us as our inheritances. God will allow situations to test our hearts, revealing our true motivation, to see if our real desire is to follow Him. The key to Ruth's decision is revealed in the words, "she was steadfastly minded to go with her" (Ruth 1:18). She would not be dissuaded from her decision by her mother-in-law's protests or her sister's decision to stay in Moab. In a real sense, it was Naomi's initial decision to return to the House of Bread that turned the disciplining hand of God to a hand of blessing for both herself and Ruth, but it was Ruth's response that made that blessing an ultimate reality for both their lives.

Ruth's Treaty

Perhaps we cannot fully appreciate Ruth's idyllic love story until we analyze the treaty that eventually brought to her such good fortune. By treaty I do not mean a legal document, but the choices Ruth made before God. Those choices influenced her future as much as any legal treaty would have. Throughout the book of Ruth, we are made aware of the power of our choices for blessing or for ill. How could our own futures be altered if, through our choices, we pursued the godly principles revealed in this courageous lady's treaty?

Ruth's declaration to follow her mother-in-law rang out clearly of true commitment. It revealed a determination to face whatever the future held for her together with her mother-in-law. I have an idea Ruth sat down somewhere and counted the cost. Was it going to be worth it to leave her land and her kindred to go to a place she'd never been, just on the strength of what she had heard?

Ruth not only tried on the "dress of consecration" but was also willing to pay the cost of the garment on the "price tag," demonstrated by her decision to follow Naomi. In order for each of us to experience the divine restoration that Ruth experienced, we must be able to say with that same determination, "live or die, sink or swim, come what may, I have decided to follow Jesus."

When Ruth left the land of Moab, she didn't know what to expect. She had never heard of Boaz; she didn't know she would be invited to eat at his table; she never dreamed of lying at his feet, or becoming his bride. She simply responded to the challenge to leave all and go to Bethlehem-judah out of her love for Naomi and Naomi's God. She was willing to become a servant in order to go to the place of God's presence. So Ruth left her homeland with utter abandonment, willing to do whatever was necessary to ensure her precious relationship with Naomi and Naomi's God.

In contrast to Orpah's decision to stay in Moab which kept her from the presence of God, Ruth's choice to follow her mother-in-law to Bethlehem-judah opened an incredible destiny to her. Ruth received the divine promises of restoration because she chose to follow the living God at the cost of breaking earthly ties and enduring the uncertainty of an unknown future in a foreign land.

Ruth's Sevenfold Declaration

Ruth's treaty was a sevenfold declaration that revealed her heart's determination. The key words in Ruth's treaty were "I will." These two words expressed the intent of her heart and formed the basis of her decision. As we observe Orpah's tearful decision not to follow Naomi, we understand that Ruth's choice was not based on emotion or sentiment, but on a decision of her will.

Decision itself is exhilarating and refreshing. Some people never know the joys and delights of walking with God because they do not choose to make decisions in favor of God, His Word and His ways. Decisive people are seldom the subjects of continued despair; they are steadfastly minded. As we decide to follow God's will, our decision will have wonderful results in our lives, as Ruth's did.

The treaty of "I wills" made by Ruth consists of these seven elements:

1. Whither thou goest, I will go (Ruth 1:16)

2. Where thou lodgest, I will lodge (Ruth 1:16)

3. Thy people shall be my people (Ruth 1:16)

4. And thy God my God (Ruth 1:16)

5. Where thou diest, will I die (Ruth 1:17)

6. And there will I be buried (Ruth 1:17)

7. The Lord do so to me, and more also, if aught but death part thee and me (Ruth 1:17)

This last "I will," though not explicitly expressed, is understood, for Ruth was declaring in essence, "I will seal this treaty with a covenant: The Lord do so to me and more also if aught but death part thee and me."

Ruth's resolve is a classic for all of literature. As an expression of love and loyalty, these words cannot be surpassed. Here is supreme devotion; here is love to the uttermost, not only passionately expressed, but as history declares, determinedly fulfilled. The beauty of its form and the utter devotion of a genuine and self-conquering love has made Ruth's vow one which never shall be forgotten. The secret of such love and loyalty is kinship in the matters of the soul and of eternity. There can be no true love, no lasting loyalty, without this kinship of soul and spirit.

Ruth's vow has stamped itself indelibly on the heart of the church. Believers throughout history have followed her example in choosing to live, and die, for God alone. How many have gained their courage to face martyrdom from reading the testimony of Ruth!

Like Ruth, we should resolve to pursue God to the end, casting our lot with the separated, sanctified people of God, cleaving to the eternal God of the Bible. Like Ruth we should enter God's field and be willing to serve. Like Ruth, we should abandon ourselves to our glorious, heavenly "Boaz," and stay at His feet until morning.

1. "I will go."

Though many people become attached to temporal things such as houses, lands and personal relationships, the eternal reality is that home is wherever the will of God is for our lives. That is where we enjoy the comfort and security of the presence of God. As much as I travel, I don't have any problem feeling at home wherever I am because I know travel is the will of God for me. The soul of man can finally shout *Home, sweet, home,* when it has found its true rest in the will of God.

I'd rather be living in a tent in Africa, knowing it was the will of God for me, than to be in a penthouse in New York City out of the will of God. My soul can never find rest and peace outside the will of God, no matter what temporal comforts would dictate to the contrary.

As we listen to Ruth say, "Whither thou goest, I will go," we witness one of the many examples of faith decisions in the Scriptures. "I will go" was the resolve of Ruth as she nestled close to the bosom of Naomi. The psalmist David declared, "I will go in the strength of the Lord" (Ps. 71:16) as he set out to witness for his God. "I will go" was the response of the prophet, Elijah, as he set out with the sons of the prophets to enlarge the school of the prophets (2 Kin. 6:3). "I will go" was also the determination of a selfish Samson as he lay himself on the lap of the deceitful and deceiving Delilah (Judg. 16:20). "I will go" was the brave decision of the beautiful Deborah as she started to fight the battles of the Lord (Judg. 4:9). "I will surely go" was the response of Rebekah as she unselfishly risked all she had to be the bride of Issac (Gen. 24:58). "I will arise and go" was the heart decision of the prodigal son as he headed for his father's house (Luke 15:18). These and many other examples underscore the power of our choices for good or ill, to affect our lives for eternity.

2. "I will lodge."

Ruth then strengthened her "I will go" by declaring, "Where you lodgest, I will lodge." She was not planning to go on vacation, with Naomi, or to try it out to see if she liked the change. Ruth's choice to renounce her homeland and cut all human ties to her own people required profound commitment. Such a decision is no small matter even today in our mobile culture. I wonder if we can comprehend the magnitude of that decision for a young widow in the culture of that day?

3. "Thy people shall be my people."

Ruth embraced the people of God in her heart when she said, "Thy people shall be my people." Two points are perfectly plain from this statement. Ruth realized that in order to enjoy Canaan and its fruits, and possess the land in its fullness, she must make the God of Naomi, the God of Abraham, Isaac and Jacob, her one and only God, and make God's people her people. She realized that she could not go with a holy God without also going with the holy people of God. These were God's separate, peculiar, and at times, persecuted people. She understood that if she were to follow the one true God, she must separate herself from the idolatrous crowd of Moab. The holy people of

God were to be her people, and the holy God her God. It is impossible to fellowship with God and refuse fellowship with the people of God. To love God is to love His people, to love the brethren, unite with them and fellowship with them.

4. "Thy God shall be my God."

The famine had done its worst. Elimelech and his two sons were dead. Ruth was a widow. She possessed little more of earthly goods than the clothing she wore on her back when she left Moab. She nevertheless possessed that which money cannot buy — a genuine modesty, virtue and a loveable nature. Her decision was prompt, firm, determined and final. Her earthly and worldly associations were sacrificed. Her mind was made up. Her heart was fixed: "Thy God shall be my God." What lovely surprises were in store for her based on this decision! Ruth never had cause to regret her decision, and we may be sure that she does not regret it now.

5. "Where thou diest, will I die."

Sometimes it is difficult to determine where a person's quality of character exceeds that of another person. But when a critical moment arises, the character is exposed. Orpah loved Naomi and for a time there seemed to be no difference between Orpah and Ruth's relationship with her, but when the moment of decision arrived, the difference was manifest. Orpah might kiss Naomi and weep, but Ruth resolved to live and die in

God's country with God's people and with Naomi. Ruth's decision, though unknown to her at the time, terminated her miseries of poverty and widowhood.

Ruth had settled the question of how she would live and where she would die. To win Christ and heaven, we must be steadfastly minded, not regretting our decisions or fickle in our resolve to follow God all the way.

Something more than mere human or creaturely kindness is essential in our relationship with God. Otherwise, we will follow Orpah's steps and go back to our old ways, old friends and old gods.

6. "And there will I be buried."

Even in burial, there is to be no hearkening back to the land of Moab. Her grave will be sealed among the people of God with whom she lived. Such finality is the attitude of a heart that knows and loves God and has forsaken all to follow Him. The Eastern customs of burial placed more importance on family burial grounds than our Western culture does. Ruth's treaty did not allow for any association with the old, idolatrous relationships she had before knowing the God of Naomi. It is no wonder God could honor her as He did when He saw the purity of her heart toward Him.

7. "The Lord do so to me, and more also if aught but death part thee and me."

Ruth closed this epochal decision with a most solemn oath. Here she brought the Lord's name into her declaration. As we have stated, the "I will" is understood here, prefacing the essence of her statement with the idea, "I will seal this treaty with a covenant." She intended her decision to be irrevocable, and it was. Once and for all, she intended to do it in the strength of the Lord and His name, and before His face.

What else could Naomi do, convinced that Ruth meant what she said. She gladly welcomed her to her people and her God. The divine historian has used these powerfully illustrative words, "but Ruth clave unto her" (Ruth 1:14). Indeed, Naomi herself was enriched by such a companion and friend.

The End of Our Will

Once we have willed our will to God, we don't struggle mentally or emotionally about temporal considerations such as where we live. We don't make decisions based on promises of material comforts, because we have no desire except for the will of God. As we choose to obey His will, we receive revelation of it. Jesus gave this promise of divine revelation to all who choose to obey the will of God. He declared, "If any man will do his will, he shall know of the doctrine, whether it be of God, or whether I speak of myself" (John 7:17). Too often we ask for revelation to help us decide what we should do with our futures *before* we choose to obey God. Jesus taught that it is as we obey the will of God that greater revelation of truth will be opened to us.

A legal will and testament declaring our intentions

and desires can only be executed after our death. Relating that to our Christian life, when we declare ourselves dead to our own will, choosing the will of God, we then become the will of God. We don't have to wonder what the will of God is, for His divine will is executed when we choose His will and die to ours. We are no longer the executor of our wills. We have become the recipient of God's will and purpose for us.

The psalmist gives us a wonderful understanding of the "I will" of God for the person who exchanges his own will for God's wonderful promises. He wrote:

> Because he hath set his love upon me, therefore will I deliver him: I will set him on high, because he hath known my name. He shall call upon me, and I will answer him: I will be with him in trouble; I will deliver him, and honour him. With long life will I satisfy him, and show him my salvation (Ps. 91:14-16).

These wonderful promises belong to believers who dare to make a treaty of their wills, promising to live only for the will of God. According to the psalmist, not only will they have God's presence in time of trouble, they will experience His deliverance, receive honor and enjoy long life while experiencing the salvation of God.

The End of Commitment

Ruth's commitment as expressed in her seven-fold treaty showed that she had indeed set her love on God. That is why He could eventually bless her with such favor and honor. Many Christians have never made the depth of commitment to God that Ruth made. There are those who have been saved since their youth and have an appreciation for the blood of Jesus, thanking Him for their salvation, but still don't know what it means to set their love on Him. They have not yielded their wills to Him so completely that they can receive the divine promises given for those who do. Many are trapped in a denominational, religious tradition that does not teach them to desire a love relationship with their Bridegroom. But God is beginning to open the hearts of many of these sincere Christians to a desire for a love relationship with Jesus. That relationship comes out of complete surrender to Him. It alone will truly satisfy their hearts.

The cry of the church for intimate relationship with the living God is heard prophetically in Ruth's commitment to Naomi and to Naomi's God. Ruth had chosen to serve the living God of Abraham, Isaac and Jacob. He is a God of holiness, the only true God. The church must decide, as Naomi and Ruth did, to return to the place of God's presence, turning from the idolatry of the land and choosing to live in the promised land, in order for her cry for relationship to be answered. She must cut all ties to the carnal way of life that surrounds her and abandon herself in utter trust to the living God. Only then will she receive the blessings of relationship with her heavenly Bridegroom and enjoy fruitfulness in His kingdom.

Having made her commitment, Ruth accompanied Naomi to Bethlehem-judah. All the city came to meet them, asking in dismay, "Is this Naomi?" This woman who had left years earlier with her husband and two sons must have seemed like a stranger to them, yet at the same time, familiar. As we have mentioned, Naomi's response to their question as to her identity was not very positive. She asked them not to call her Naomi, but to call her Mara, declaring, "for the Almighty hath dealt very bitterly with me" (Ruth 1:20). By that she indicated that she was not the same woman who had left Bethlehem-judah.

Whatever her emotional state, the important thing was that Naomi was home where God could continue His redemption in her life. It is interesting to note that Naomi was never called Mara in the Scriptures. God intended that she be called Naomi. He would restore to her the pleasantness of His presence in the House of Bread. Though she was faced with humble new beginnings, the hand of God on her life that had disciplined her severely would now bring her into great blessing.

Neither Naomi nor Ruth would have known complete redemption if they had not been willing in the time of testing to make a complete commitment to serve the living God. Perhaps we cannot fully appreciate the courage it took for Ruth to abandon herself to the will of God as she did, for we know the end of the story. She knew only that she could not abandon her love for Naomi's God. As we follow the narrative to see Ruth discover her kinsman-redeemer, unfolding God's wonderful purpose for her, we should take courage in the complete surrender of our own lives in utter abandon to the will of God. He has promised to secure our futures in the same way He did Ruth's.

After Naomi and Ruth arrived in Bethlehem-judah, a subtle shift in the narrative brings Ruth into focus as the main character of the story, indicated by the title of the book. From this point on, we witness the exciting events that bring Ruth into enviable circumstances of great prominence and joyful security as a bride of a wealthy lord of Israel. Considering what was involved in Ruth's obedience to bring her to this place of preeminence and honor as the bride of Boaz, we will understand what we must be willing to do to come into such an intimate relationship with our heavenly Bridegroom.

Such a wonderful love story can be ours as well if we choose to come into relationship with our Kinsman-Redeemer, serving Him with a heart filled with humble gratitude and love. The constitution of the kingdom (the Beatitudes) declares, "Blessed are the poor in spirit: for theirs is the kingdom of heaven" (Matt. 5:3). Being poor in spirit simply means we are humble enough to acknowledge our need of God. In that acknowledgment, God will provide for us what we need to fulfill His purposes for us. 🌱

6

*Tenderness Toward
the Helpless*

The Law of Moses, given to the children of
Israel by God, made provision for the
redemption of the poor. It stated that if
someone became so poor that he could not pay
his debts, he could sell his land and/or himself to
pay his debtors. How much he sold depended on
the extent of his debt. Even after he was sold,
however, he retained a right of redemption (Lev.
25:48-54).

There were three ways, according to the Law,

that a man who had succumbed to poverty could redeem himself and his land. First, if he could accumulate enough to buy back his land, he was free to do so (Lev. 25:26-27; 49-50). Secondly, if he could not buy back his land, he would have to work as a hired hand until the year of Jubilee, celebrated every fifty years. At that time all property was returned to its original owner and all who had sold themselves and their property could return to their land (Lev. 25:28,54). How anxiously everyone awaited the Jubilee when all mortgages were canceled, and those who had succumbed to poverty were given a second chance!

The third way a man could be redeemed was if one of his brothers or another blood relative who had the means to pay the price of redemption would purchase what his indebted relative had sold (Lev. 25:47-53). According to this law, it was the responsibility of a near kinsman to come and buy back what his relative had sold (Lev. 25:25) Boaz indicates this fact by stating there is a nearer kinsman than he, to whom he is obligated to appeal before offering redemption to Ruth. In the case of a widow who had no son to care for her, it became the responsibility of the brother of the deceased husband to marry her, redeem her lost inheritance and raise up seed for his brother's house (Deut. 25:5-10). For the Israelite, these laws could not be treated as mere suggestions for proper conduct. If they were not strictly obeyed, those who violated them would have consequences to pay.

Naomi was both a victim of poverty and of the

loss of her husband and sons. The laws of redemption we have described made provision for a widow in Israel. Though her plight seemed desperate, Naomi knew there was a means of redemption provided for her according to the Law of Moses. In type, these laws foreshadow the wonderful, eternal redemption that Christ has provided for mankind.

Relationship of Choice

The church has not been bought with silver or gold, but with the precious blood of Jesus that made atonement for our sins. Through His sacrifice at Calvary, God has redeemed us from the curse of sin with its death and destruction. Because of Adam and Eve's disobedience to God's command, they were separated from relationship with God. As a result of that separation, they not only lost their innocence, they lost the privilege of maturing in the character of God. They never realized the purpose of God for mankind, to become sons of God bearing His image.

Though eternal salvation is ours as we accept the sacrifice of Christ for our sins, the *maturity* which reflects His character in our lives comes only as we choose to live in obedience to Him. As we accept salvation through Christ, we are again given the power and privilege of choosing to be obedient to His Word. As we learn to walk in that obedience, we are transformed into His image. As we commit our lives to His will, we enter into the love relationship that He intended for Adam and

Eve to enjoy. Only then will we have the character of God formed in us, bringing us to maturity.

It is this maturity of which the apostle Paul speaks: "until we all attain to the unity of the faith, and of the knowledge of the Son of God, to a mature man, to the measure of the stature which belongs to the fulness of Christ" (Eph. 4:13, NAS). Our relationship of love and obedience to God brings us to maturity in our Christian character and qualifies us to become a part of the bride of Christ. Becoming a bride is not by appointment; it is a love relationship of choice. Love for our Redeemer fills our hearts and makes us willing to forsake all to belong to Him. In that choice to forsake all, we find the key to our complete restoration.

Covenant Promises

Naomi and Ruth's story is not one of happenstance or good fortune. Centuries earlier, God had provided for their redemption in the covenant He gave to Moses. God made provision for their redemption before their birth so that when they acknowledged their need to be redeemed, they could enter into His provision.

So it is with us. Our redemption was provided long before our birth. The Scriptures teach that Christ was the Lamb slain from the foundation of the world (Rev. 13:8). Though there was a specific moment in history when Jesus came to earth to fulfill the plan of redemption, He was in readiness to fulfill that plan for all eternity. All who lived before Christ looked forward to the provision of the cross, and we who live after Christ's sacrifice on Calvary look back to that provision for our salvation. For us to enjoy our complete restoration in Christ, we have only to choose, as Naomi and Ruth did, to turn our feet toward the place provided for our redemption, continually yielding our lives to His plan for us.

God can, and does, intervene in our lives sovereignly. The Scriptures teach that we love God because He loved us first (1 John 4:19). We could not come to Him except He draws us (John 6:44). God initiates His work of grace in our lives. Having said that, however, it is also true that we must acknowledge our need of Him in order to find Him. When Jesus declared, "Blessed are the poor in spirit: for theirs is the kingdom of heaven" (Matt. 5:3), He was referring to that deep inner sense of need that causes us to cry out to God. When we do that, we will find the whole kingdom of heaven at our disposal.

Humble Beginnings

Upon her return to Bethlehem-judah, Naomi was faced with the shame of poverty in a city where, as Elimelech's wife, she once lived as a wealthy woman. She had come back possessing nothing, faced with hunger and bearing the reproach of widowhood. Ruth, well aware of their social and economic plight, had chosen to share an uncertain future with her mother-in-law.

Upon reaching Bethlehem-judah, Naomi and Ruth's first concern was to find food for their sustenance. Evidently understanding the provision of the law for the poor, Ruth asked permission of Naomi to go to the fields to glean what she could for their food. Gleaners did not receive wages as the reapers did but, according to the law, were allowed to keep the grain they gathered for their own needs.

The reapers harvested their fields by thrusting their sickles into the standing grain. However, they did not go into the corners of the fields, nor retrieve what was accidentally dropped in the process of harvesting. The law declared that these portions were to be left for the poor who came to glean what the reapers left in order to live. Ruth was among the poor that morning as she looked for a field in which to glean in the season of barley harvest.

No Happenstance!

The simple little phrase, "and her hap was to light on a part of the field belonging unto Boaz" (Ruth 2:3), gives us the key to the sovereignty of God in Ruth's life. She had committed her will to the living God, and He began the beautiful orchestration of His purpose, lovingly establishing her goings. The word *hap* indicates that it was not coincidental that she found herself in the field of Boaz. It is rather an expression of prevenient grace, the sovereign working of God to direct a life that has been surrendered to Him. God's prevenient grace operates in the circumstances of our lives beyond our knowledge and takes care of us even when we don't know what is happening in the unseen world. That sovereign eye of God guided Ruth to the field of Boaz, her kinsman-redeemer.

The Redeemer

How can we describe the beauty of the word *redeemer?* Only as we receive revelation of the utter helplessness and hopelessness of our human condition without God can we fully appreciate the wonder of finding our Redeemer. Ruth was facing a life of loneliness, poverty and great difficulty as a widow in a foreign land. For Ruth, the discovery of a kinsman-redeemer would be a precious gift to bring deliverance from her desperate human plight. Each of us would be on our way to hell without the discovery of our heavenly Redeemer. We would be, in a spiritual sense, widowed, childless beggars, homeless victims of the idolatry of Moab.

There are three Hebrew words that correspond to our English word *kinsman.* The first two, *moda* and *qarob,* define a kinsman simply as "a near relative linked to us by family ties." It is the third Hebrew word, *goel,* that carries the connotation of "kinsman-redeemer." It was the *goel* who could make it possible for Ruth to experience complete restoration.

Three things were necessary for a person to be a *goel.* First, as stated, he had to be a near kinsman, having the relationship required for redemption. Second, he had to have the power to redeem, meaning the financial means to do so. And third, he had to willing to redeem, to pay the price to buy back that which was lost. Only the kinsman-redeemer had the right to buy back the property that had been sold to another.

A redeemer redeems. Continual action is indicated by the suffix *er*. For example, a farmer is one who characteristically farms, and a writer is one whose vocation is writing. So a redeemer is one who is by nature involved in the ongoing process of redemption. This understanding is important to the integrity of the word *redemption*. Redemption is not a one time act, but requires continued relationship between the redeemer and the one being redeemed. In Israel, a kinsman-redeemer was one who, by his choice, became responsible for the life of the person he redeemed as long as that person lived.

Our Heavenly *Goel*

I recently had the privilege of spending some time with a great military man of the Israeli army who had led the deliverance of the Jews out of Russia. He was visiting our church, and we ate lunch together, surrounded by his security guards. Earlier I had been privileged to be one of the Christian ministers he invited to spend a week in Israel with the heads of the Israeli government.

During a very private moment of conversation, tears streamed down this man's cheeks, as he said, "I don't understand, little lady. I feel a force coming from you and the people in your church toward me. I can't explain it, but it breaks everything in me down. I don't know what to call it, but it feels like love. You are a gentile Christian, and yet you love me, a Jew. I didn't know Christians loved Jews; I thought they hated them for crucifying their Messiah. Please explain to me how you feel about Jews."

I shot up a quick "SOS" to my Father to give me an answer for this dear man, and the Holy Spirit prompted me to say, "Sir, why should I not love you? You didn't kill my Messiah. No man did. He chose to give His life for me willingly. No man took His life from Him. Yes, I do love you and all Jewish people. That is the force you are feeling."

That evening, when this great Israeli leader had finished speaking to our church concerning the Israeli government, I said to him, "Sir, I sense that your heart is very near the kingdom of God. I want you to know that the God of Abraham that you serve is our God. And you and I will come into the kingdom through the same covenant because Jews and gentiles alike have been redeemed by the blood of Jesus Christ, who willingly became our heavenly *Goel.*" In those tender moments that precious Jewish man was brought very close to a revelation of his Messiah.

In order to worship our Bridegroom as God desires, our spirits need a revelation of the great sacrifice Jesus made to become our *Goel*, our Kinsman-Redeemer. Christ, the spotless Lamb of God, had the necessary relationship to the Father for redemption. He had the means of redemption, having humbled Himself to become a man, a servant of men. Yet, having the relationship and the means required for redemption was not enough to redeem mankind. There had to be a willingness to pay the awful price of our salvation—crucifixion on the cross. As we behold the unspeakable love of the Lamb of God who willingly chose to redeem us, the church is going to be restored to a higher realm of worship than we have ever experienced.

When the Holy Spirit opened John the Revelator's eyes to see the worship of heaven, he beheld the Lamb that was slain as the One who was worthy of worship and able to open the book. He saw the elders bowing before the Lamb and singing a new song: "Thou art worthy to take the book, and to open the seals thereof: for thou wast slain, and hast redeemed us to God by thy blood out of every kindred, and tongue, and people, and nation" (Rev. 5:9). Though Christ was proclaimed as the Lion of the tribe of Judah in that same heavenly scene, it was as the slain Lamb that He stepped forth to take the book. We worship our Kinsman-Redeemer as the Lamb who was slain from the foundation of the world. Beholding the Lamb of God as our lovely Redeemer will always evoke our highest worship!

The Scriptures declare that "for the joy that was set before him" (Heb. 12:2). Jesus endured the cross. Jesus Himself declared, "I am the good shepherd: the good shepherd giveth his life for the sheep...I lay down my life for the sheep" (John 10:11,15). Willingly and joyfully He laid down His life to become our Redeemer. As we have seen, a *goel* redeems by choosing to become responsible for another's life. It is inaccurate to think of Jesus as our Redeemer simply in terms of One who initially forgave our sins and blotted out our transgressions. Christ, our Redeemer, has a continuing love relationship of choice with His redeemed ones that we will cultivate throughout eternity.

Not by Works

It is not by our works that we are redeemed but by the precious blood of Jesus. That efficacious, vicarious, substitutionary, mediatorial sacrifice has never been polluted or diluted but is just as powerful today as the day Christ died on Calvary. The apostle Peter declared, "Ye know that ye were not redeemed with corruptible things, as silver and gold, from your vain conversation received by tradition from your fathers; But with the precious blood of Christ, as of a lamb without blemish and without spot" (1 Pet. 1:18-19). As we worship God, beholding the Lamb, His blood will become more and more precious to us.

The blood was so precious in the Old Testament tabernacle that cherubims were set over the holy of holies where the blood was sprinkled (1 Kin. 8:3-7). These heavenly representatives, though only types of the reality they foreshadowed, focused man's attention on the value of the blood sacrifice. It is the redemptive blood of Jesus, not our own works, that gives us divine life every day because He was willing to become our *goel*. Boaz foreshadowed this wonderful provision of our heavenly *Goel* in the life of Ruth.

Tender Watchings

Ruth found herself in the field of Boaz, her kinsman-redeemer, though she did not know it at the time. She did not know who he was, nor that he had the power to redeem her from her unhappy situation. She had not met him or seen him face-to-face. She didn't know that he would feed her or generously give her drink, nor that she would find grace in his eyes. She was aware only of her hunger and of the provision of the Law that allowed her to glean in the land where there was a great harvest.

As Ruth worked in the heat of the sun, her diligence did not go unnoticed. One day Boaz himself saw her and asked his servant about her. Her willingness to take the lowly place of gleaner to provide food for her mother-in-law must have been the talk of the town. It seems that everyone knew she had left her family and homeland to live in a foreign land and care for her mother-in-law.

I imagine Boaz walking through the sheaves of grain, looking over the field, when all of the sudden he was attracted to someone who seemed to be a little different from most of the reapers. He began to notice the way she walked and talked. He became interested enough to ask about her. She was different — she was Moabitish. She seemed determined. Boaz spoke to the servant in charge of the reapers, asking who this girl was.

After hearing his servant's response, Boaz

turned his attention directly toward Ruth. From the moment Boaz approached Ruth, he showed that he was impressed with what he had heard of her commitment to her mother-in-law, admiring the trust in God it displayed. Greeting her, he told her to remain in his field where he had secured her protection. She was to drink from the vessels which the young men had drawn.

Ruth could not hide her surprise at hearing his generous offer. Bowing to the ground, she asked why she had found grace in his eyes, knowing she was a stranger. Ruth's spontaneous response revealed the true humility of her heart. She did not regard herself worthy of such favor.

Boaz responded to her question, saying:

> It hath fully been shown me, all that thou hast done unto thy mother-in-law since the death of thine husband: and how thou hast left thy father and thy mother, and the land of thy nativity, and art come unto a people which thou knewest not heretofore. The Lord recompense thy work, and a full reward be given thee of the Lord God of Israel, under whose wings thou **art** come to trust (Ruth 2:11-12).

As Christians, we can expect such approval and personal attention from our Redeemer when we seek to satisfy our hunger in His "field." Hearing His voice as He welcomes us into His kingdom and reassures us of His intentions toward us is the most comforting experience we can have on earth.

May we respond as Ruth did when we hear the beloved voice of our Redeemer and wonder how we have found such favor when we are aliens and strangers to His kingdom of light and love.

I imagine Ruth working in the field the rest of that day singing "Amazing Grace, how sweet the sound, that saved a wretch like me." When we find ourselves in a place of hunger, gleaning for our life, we are very thankful to be accepted into the field where we can find adequate provision to feed that hunger. Seeking to satisfy our hunger for the living Word, we are grateful for every handful of truth that satisfies our hearts.

Revelation of the Word

Jesus declared in the face of Satan, "It is written, Man shall not live by bread alone, but by every word that proceedeth out of the mouth of God" (Matt. 4:4). He also declared Himself to be the living Word, the heavenly Manna. God doesn't intend for us to understand His Word in theory through the power of the intellect. He wants the Scriptures to come alive to our hearts through revelation by the Holy Spirit, so we see Jesus, our heavenly *Goel*, on every page.

As we take time to meditate on the Word, Jesus becomes more real to our hearts, and we are filled with His life. He tells us not to seek nourishment anywhere else; He is all we need. Jesus declared, "I am the way, the truth, and the life" (John 14:6). He is the "Alpha and Omega" (Rev. 1:8). He is the "author and finisher of our faith" (Heb. 12:2). In

Him alone can we find rest for our souls and all that we need for life.

As we commit our lives to obey Him with all our hearts, revelation of the Word will be ours. The Scriptures will come alive to our hearts by revelation. When the Holy Spirit, through our obedience to Him, becomes our divine Teacher, we will get a personal glimpse of our "Boaz." Revelation will continue to increase, never ceasing unless we willfully take ourselves out of the place of obedience. The revelation which has begun in our hearts here on earth will continue throughout eternity. As we stay in the Word, revelation becomes our "home" in God. It is there that we will find true rest for our souls that nothing of this world can provide.❦

7

The Treatment of Ruth

We can safely conclude that Boaz was favorably impressed with the Moabitish girl he found gleaning in his fields by the way he spoke to her and the preferential treatment he gave her over his other handmaidens. The attitude of wealthy landowners toward gleaners in that culture was usually one of tolerance. Gleaners would not expect to be spoken to by the landowner, much less welcomed to his field. Boaz had not only commended Ruth for her care of her mother-in-law and invited her to stay in his fields, he also offered her the privilege of drinking the water that his young men had carried. He commanded them to respect her person, promising to protect her from any harm.

The Process of Redemption

Such personal attention was regarded by all as highly unusual preferential treatment. As we look closely at the kind of treatment Boaz offered Ruth in contrast to what would have been expected according to the customs of the day, we gain deep appreciation for the heart of this kinsman-redeemer. Allegorically, we glimpse the loving heart of our great Redeemer.

When Ruth asked Boaz why she had found such grace in his eyes, he did not comment on her nationality, social status or her poverty. Rather, his response showed that he was impressed with her character, her choices and the consistency of her life. He understood that her desire for the living God had caused her to put her trust in Him. Her devotion had won his admiration.

In that same way, our heavenly Kinsman-Redeemer values and responds to our desire for Him and our devotion to Him. He does not condemn us because of our unworthiness as strangers to dwell with Him. He loves us for the choices we have made to follow Him. We find grace in His eyes as we continually come to "glean" truth and life from Him for ourselves and for others in need.

The Provision of Water

Gleaners did not expect landowners to provide water for them, but Boaz offered Ruth the water drawn by his young men. The source of water could have been a long way off from the field. Perhaps Ruth had only the water she could carry from home to last her during the long hours of toil under the hot sun. Whatever the case, it was an unusual kindness for a wealthy landowner like Boaz to make such a generous offer to a gleaner.

Allegorically, this provision of water is very significant. Our minds reach forward to another time and place when a Samaritan woman was offered water unexpectedly by a man she did not know. Jesus offered her living water that would satisfy her thirst in such a way that she would never thirst again. He said it would be "a well of water springing up into everlasting life" (John 4:14). Unwittingly, this woman had a private audience with her Redeemer.

It is a well-known fact that without water we can only live a short time. Jesus readily used the analogy of water to represent His divine presence filling those who believed, satisfying their thirst and springing up inside them like a well. Throughout the Scriptures, saints can be tracked by following their altars and wells. Altars of worship marked their journeys, and wells providing the water vital to life were dug everywhere they went.

The church needs to be a place where altars of commitment and worship are built and wells of water are dug in our own lives to sustain us and provide life for others. For that to be a reality, our lives must be continually surrendered to the Holy Spirit and filled with His life-giving presence as we live in daily prayer and in the Word of God.

The Promise of Protection

Boaz also commanded his young men not to insult or make improper advances toward Ruth, nor to reproach or rebuke her. This promise of protection released Ruth from fear of harm and gave her peace of mind as she gleaned among the men in the field. For Ruth, a widow who was a stranger in the land without hope of protection, this promise must have especially comforted her heart.

The church offers believers this same comfort of protection from the baser elements of the world. Christ is the head of the church, and Christians are admonished to have His mind of humility and love toward one another. We are taught throughout the epistles to treat each other with careful concern, watching out for one another's interests (Phil. 2:3-4). The church should be a safe place where people can come to find solace and comfort from the evils of the world.

Handfuls on Purpose

Next, Boaz invited this Moabitish gleaner to sit beside the reapers at meal time and eat the bread provided for them. Such an invitation went against the protocol of that culture completely. Perhaps it is this offer that Boaz made to Ruth that convinces us his interest in her was more than casual. He gave her parched corn as she sat at the table with him. In this way he was showing he had a personal interest in her. We saw earlier this interest by his ordering handfuls on purpose dropped unexpectedly for her by the servant. As Boaz ate with Ruth, he demonstrated a more personal interest in her to those around him.

His next command confirmed that interest. When Ruth left the table to return to the field, Boaz told his young men to allow her to glean among the sheaves and to drop handfuls of barley on purpose for her. As we have said, gleaners were generally confined to the corners of the fields and to the areas of the field where the reapers had already removed the sheaves. Gleaning among the sheaves was not allowed. Bible commentators agree that Boaz's command to let Ruth glean among the sheaves was not simply a sign of his generosity and compassion toward the poor. Rather it showed that he felt a peculiar interest in Ruth, who had won his heart by her humility, her faithful attachment to her mother-in-law and her love to the God of Israel.[1]

Our Redeemer desires to show us this kind of personal attention and preferential treatment. As we feed on His Word and sit in His presence, He loves to give us handfuls of revelation that feed and strengthen our souls. He gives us an abundant supply to take to others. Such special treatment reveals the heart of our Redeemer toward the helpless who are struggling in their unhappy human misery. Though Boaz was not acting officially as Ruth's kinsman-redeemer in these present kindnesses, his redeemer heart was filled with desire to make her difficult situation easier to bear.

It is worth our pausing to reflect on what might have happened if Ruth had not been willing to become a gleaner. She would certainly have missed this opportunity to win the heart of the wealthy landowner, dining with him at his table. As believers, we should never shrink from taking the low place, seeking to serve others. In this way, we will be sure to attract the attention of our Redeemer who will show us undeserved kindnesses.

Provision Shared

At the end of the day, Ruth hurried home to Naomi with her arms full of grain and her heart full of gratitude and joy. As they rehearsed the events of the day, Ruth was only aware of the comfort and relief she had felt in being able to glean without fear. She was grateful for the help given her. Naomi recognized the hand of the Lord upon Ruth's endeavors. Naomi knew that there was far more available from this man than simply a comfortable situation for gleaning.

A Higher Law

One of the most blessed verses in the Bible is the verse describing Boaz: "And Naomi had a kinsman of her husband's, a mighty man of wealth, of the family of Elimelech; and his name was Boaz" (Ruth 2:1). He is described here as a mighty man which meant he was a hero or chief. Boaz was not a common man. We see him here as a man of grace. As such, he becomes the outstanding character in the story, next to Ruth. As we will discuss in more detail later in the book, Boaz proved himself to be a friend in need to Naomi and to Ruth. It was well for Naomi that she had such a friend as he.

The significance of Boaz's role is heightened as we understand the levirate law that was followed in Israel during that time. The root word of levirate is *levir* which actually means "husband's brother." According to the levirate law, when a married man died without any surviving children, it was customary for the deceased man's brother to take the widow as his wife. The children from this union counted as children of the first husband. The law applied to brothers who lived together, allowing the survived brother the option of refusing (Deut. 25:5-10).[2]

The book of Ruth reveals that there was a nearer kinsman who should have married Ruth, according to levirate law. The law would not have required Boaz to follow through with the redemption since there was a nearer kinsman. Yet the heart of Boaz was listening to a higher law — the law of love. He proved his friendship by his willingness to provide redemption for this foreign girl, taking her as his bride though she was not of the house of Israel.

Allegorically, it follows that we have been eternally blessed because Almighty God became our friend, our hero, our Redeemer, though we were foreigners to His kingdom. Christ proved His friendship to us, being willing to do all we need for our redemption. He lived and died to show us this higher law of grace revealed through love.

As we have seen, the family name of Elimelech meant "God is my King." Boaz represented his family well, typifying Christ who is God, our coming King.

The name, Boaz, can be translated "in him is strength." He was able to demonstrate that strength for Ruth and Naomi, and restore all their possessions and inheritance. In Christ we see the strength to accomplish all the purposes of God for mankind in this earth, bringing the grace of God to all who will receive it.

Boaz was also characterized by grace. Ruth desired and needed to find grace in someone's eyes. She said to Naomi, "Let me now go to the field, and glean ears of corn after him in whose sight I shall find grace" (Ruth 2:2). God led her in His kind providence to glean in the part of the field that belonged to Boaz. It seemed a chance circumstance, but conclusion of the matter proved that God was in it.

This grace that characterized Boaz was seen in the way he greeted his servants, as well as the way they received him. Coming into the field, he said to them, "The Lord be with you" (Ruth 2:4). And they answered him, "The Lord bless thee" (Ruth 2:4). (Most labor troubles would cease if such a relationship existed today between employer and employees.) It is a significant revelation of the grace of his character that Boaz asked his servant about Ruth when he saw her in his field. Ruth was astonished at the grace of Boaz that brought such a response to her and her plight.

Today, men of Boaz's type are needed everywhere. Thousands of people are in need of someone simply to acknowledge them, to inquire about them and to encourage them. In our relationship to Christ, it is His gracious acknowledgement of our person and our plight that inspires our love for Him.

Grace is not merely a theological term that describes the new covenant superseding the Law of Moses. Grace is the wonderful redemptive response of love that is not required by law. It is when one stoops from his position to extend comfort and help to one who is not worthy. This higher law of grace was working in Boaz, foreshadowing the love of our Savior that caused Him to sacrifice His life to redeem mankind. Because of the grace working in Boaz, though he was not strictly bound by the levirate law, he chose to redeem Ruth.

When Ruth told her mother-in-law that she had been gleaning in Boaz's field, I have an idea that Naomi was startled. At the mention of his name, her response was: "The man is near of kin unto us, one of our next kinsmen" (Ruth 2:20). The word *kin* (qarob in Hebrew) is used to mean a relative. She commented to Ruth that Boaz was one of her husband's relatives. But when Naomi said *kinsman,* it signified that Naomi understood Ruth had found grace in Boaz's eyes. The word *kinsman* is a completely different word in the Hebrew from the word *kin*. Kinsman is the word *goel* in Hebrew that we defined earlier. In the Authorized Version of the Bible, the note in the margin referring to *goel* reads, "One that hath the right to redeem."

So in Christ, we have found not only a relative, in that He chose to empty Himself to become a human being (Phil. 2:7-8), but a *goel* who has the right to redeem us because of His willingness to live a sinless life in relation to His Father. That purity of character allowed Him to offer Himself as the spotless Lamb required to take away the sin of the world. Grace was perfectly personified in Christ, our heavenly Boaz, our divine *Goel*, who offered Himself as a perfect sacrifice for our sins by the shedding of His blood. Boaz is a beautiful Old Testament picture of the grace of God ever reaching out to mankind.

Our Heavenly Boaz

In the church today, we are even now receiving the kindnesses of our heavenly Boaz. Our Redeemer is comforting us and protecting us from harm, giving us handfuls on purpose for ourselves and others. But there is a new day dawning for the church. She will have restored to her all that she lost because of famine. The church will come into a greater relationship with her Redeemer than she has ever known. Those who have suffered the consequences of famine and are willing to turn in repentance and come home as Naomi did are going to find great grace in the eyes of their Redeemer.

Can you imagine the sight of Naomi, an old widow woman, stooped, aged, wrinkled, humiliated and disgraced because no one has stepped forward to redeem her? There was no one in Moab to buy her back. There was no one who could give her a son in her old age, and the sons of her youth were dead. Now she was back home in Bethlehem-judah with her widowed Moabitess daughter-in-law. Out of such desolation, what hope must have sprung up in Naomi's heart as Ruth told her of the kindness of Boaz. Naomi knew that he was a near kinsman who had the power to redeem them!

The world has seen the church in its widow's garb for too long, recognizing her by her mournful appearance. We have lost many of our sons and daughters to the land of "Moab" because of the famine of our own hearts. Our lifelessness and lack of joy has "turned off" many young people to any desire for the things of God. We have wept because we don't have a Boaz, a redeemer, to buy back the land we lost during the famine. We have become poor beggars, dressed in widow's garbs, living in the land with no rights and without sons to care for us.

As Christians, our hope lies in the fact that as we return to the House of Bread, we will discover a field that belongs to our Kinsman-Redeemer in which to glean. As we take the place of a gleaner willingly, our Redeemer notices us and extends His kindnesses. We enjoy His provision and feel the safety of His protection. Before long, we will even find ourselves dining in His presence, a significant precursor to our complete restoration.

Fullness of Time

Naomi understood the way of redemption according to the Law of Moses. Her only immediate instructions to Ruth were to stay in the field of Boaz with his other handmaidens, as he had commanded her. So Ruth continued to glean in the field of Boaz until the end of the barley and wheat harvests.

The narrative does not tell us why Naomi waited to present to Ruth her plan for seeking rest for her daughter-in-law. Surely a wonderful hope had filled her heart when Ruth told her where she had gleaned and the kindness with which Boaz had treated her. But we understand from the Scriptures that there is always a time element involved in redemption, and Naomi seemed to be awaiting the opportune time. She knew the ways of her people, and she waited for the time when Boaz would be rejoicing in the bountiful harvest as they preserved the grain at the threshing floor.

Though Naomi confided to Ruth that Boaz was a near kinsman, she gave her no other instructions except to stay in the field of Boaz. Again, the obedience of Ruth is revealed by the statement, "So she kept fast by the maidens of Boaz to glean unto the end of barley harvest and of wheat harvest; and dwelt with her mother-in-law" (Ruth 2:23). What rewards obedience brings to the lives of the those who are willing to commit their ways to God!✿

8

Tarrying for the Appointment

*R*uth had worked diligently for many
weeks, gleaning throughout both the
barley and the wheat harvests in the field
of Boaz. Now that the harvest was finished, the
reapers were busy preserving the grain that had
been gathered at the threshing floor. Sheaves of
harvested grain had been stacked in huge piles
there. The threshing floors in Palestine were
nothing more than level places in the field out
under the open heaven that had been stamped

quite hard. In the evenings, a cool wind would rise, and the harvesters would take advantage of that breeze to winnow their grain. The harvesters stayed there day and night until the grain was safely winnowed and stored.[1]

Naomi knew that Boaz could be found on the threshing floor, winnowing the harvested grain until late at night.

> Then Naomi her mother-in-law said unto her, My daughter, shall I not seek rest for thee, that it may be well with thee? (Ruth 3:1).

Naomi shared with Ruth her plan to seek redemption through Boaz, their near kinsman. Perhaps Naomi explained how Ruth could be lifted from the shame of the Moabitish heritage, have her widowhood exchanged for marriage and leave gleaning forever for the continual comfort of the presence of her redeemer husband. What a blissful thought! This little Moabitish maiden, who didn't belong in Israel, who had come to a strange land only because of her love for God, was now being offered hope of complete restoration.

The Hope of Redemption

Already Ruth had been promoted from gleaning in the corners of the field to gleaning among the sheaves. She had even been given the unusual privilege of eating at the table with Boaz. But had she dared to anticipate the possibility of being chosen by Boaz to be his bride? She had simply followed obediently the instructions given her by Naomi and Boaz to glean in his field. Her obedience would bring Ruth into a much more intimate relationship than she could have hoped for. Though she was probably not aware of it, that obedience was a prerequisite for finding the rest Naomi desired for her.

What was this rest that Naomi desired for Ruth? Was it a physical refreshing from the weariness of her hard work in the fields? Notice that Naomi didn't say, "You're tired and weary, Ruth. Please go to bed and rest." It is clear from the context that the rest Naomi was referring to was not merely physical rest. Rather, she spoke of a wonderful state of grace that Ruth had not yet known, a rest of relationship that she did not yet entered into.

In the New Testament we read, "There remaineth therefore a rest to the people of God" (Heb. 4:9). This promise also refers to a state of grace. The writer to the Hebrews was exhorting all believers to enter into the rest of God for their souls through faith. He cited the example of the Israelites who failed to enter into their inheritance in the promised land through their unbelief, never enjoying the state of grace God has promised us. Only as we, by faith, enter into intimate relationship with Christ, our great High Priest, will we know His rest. He promises a supernatural rest for our souls that is all pervasive, taking our emptiness and filling our lives with security and freedom from fear. God ordained such rest for us to enjoy from before the foundation of the world.

Jesus spoke these beautiful words to John the Revelator, "Behold, I stand at the door, and knock: if any man hear my voice, and open the door, I will come in to him, and will sup with him, and he with me" (Rev. 3:20). The word *sup* is used only three times in Scripture, and it means "communion." That is a more intimate word than we have perhaps realized, referring to the communion of the bride and bridegroom. To commune with God involves much more than casual conversation or simple petitions. True communion involves a spiritual relationship of intimate love with our Redeemer. It is a place of rest that is found only in complete surrender to our Bridegroom. In that relationship, Christ gives divine revelation, impregnating the spirit of His bride with His living Word — His life.

My one request of God before I minister to a congregation is expressed in the cry of Queen Esther: "Life me and life my people" (Esth. 7:3, author's paraphrase). My keen desire is that the life of God, conceived in my spirit through communion with Him, would flow to the people through the spoken word. The apostle Paul declared, "the letter killeth, but the spirit giveth life" (2 Cor. 3:6). Unless the Spirit of God causes the Word of God to live in us we will not be filled with the life of God.

So the rest Naomi was referring to was not simply physical rest from her hard labors, though that would also be a blessed part of her redemption. Naomi was speaking of a rest that would come from intimate relationship with her bridegroom. It involved having a secure future, one that would lift from her the reproach of widowhood and poverty and bring her into prosperity and honor. God offered this rest to His people through the prophet, Isaiah: "For thus saith the Lord God, the Holy One of Israel; In returning and rest shall ye be saved; in quietness and in confidence shall be your strength" (Is. 30:15). But those words are followed by this sad commentary: "and ye would not." We can only find that kind of security as we respond positively to God's offer of relationship with us. In this beautiful allegory, no one could give Ruth this kind of rest except Boaz. So with us, we cannot find that rest outside of relationship with Christ.

Naomi's latest instructions to Ruth would tell her how to get Boaz's attention so that she would ultimately become the recipient of all that his rest promised her. As we apply the allegorical truths that Naomi's instructions reveal to our Christian walk, we will learn what is involved in entering into true revelation of our Bridegroom-Redeemer.

Wash Thyself

Ruth needed first of all to wash herself before going to the threshing floor to seek an encounter with Boaz. This may seem a strange command to those of us accustomed to the Western culture where daily baths are the norm. But in the culture of Palestine where people did not enjoy the convenience of turning the tap for as much hot water as they desired, bathing was almost considered an "event." Water would probably have to be carried a good distance to their homes. People were accustomed to living closer to the dust of the earth and farm life than we are, and personal washing was reserved for special occasions.

In the Scriptures, washing represents a cleansing from all that pollutes our souls. The apostle Paul taught that "Christ also loved the church, and gave himself for it; That he might sanctify and cleanse it with the washing of water by the word, That he might present it to himself a glorious church, not having spot, or wrinkle, or any such thing; but that it should be holy and without blemish" (Eph. 5:25-27). In Jesus' high priestly prayer, He asked His Father to "Sanctify them through thy truth: thy word is truth" (John 17:17).

We are cleansed from sin by the blood of Christ, and we are sanctified by the washing of the water by the Word. The command for Ruth to wash herself foreshadows an important aspect of our preparation for coming into the presence of our Bridegroom-Redeemer. As we prepare our hearts for the presence of our Bridegroom, we need to allow ourselves to be washed by the water of the Word.

Anoint Thyself

Naomi then instructed Ruth to anoint herself. The method of anointing in biblical times was to rub oil on a person or object. Usually olive oil was used, though at times other oils might have been substituted. In these ancient cultures, anointing was generally for medicinal as well as cosmetic purposes.

While we cannot include a complete study of the anointing here, it is important to realize that believers are anointed not just once, but continually, as we allow the Holy Spirit to fill us with the divine fragrance of Christ. There are fourteen different anointings revealed in the Bible, which I have discussed fully in a study guide called *The Anointing*.[2] It is the anointing that destroys the yokes of bondage over our lives (Is. 10:27). As we allow ourselves to be filled continually with the anointing of the Holy Spirit, we exchange the bondage of our self-life for His divine life, and we are cleansed from the "filthiness of the flesh" (2 Cor. 7:1) that touts its own odor. If we don't experience daily washings and anointings, it won't be long until we will not be able to disguise our lack of divine life.

A clean spirit, freshly anointed, will not only bring divine revelation to our own hearts but will allow people to sense the presence of God in our lives as well. The way we talk, the attitudes with which we respond to life's situations, the love we show our family and friends — all our actions and reactions will reveal the presence of God within us, or the lack of it. There should always be a clear evidence of the anointing of the Holy Spirit in our lives. That anointing prepares us to come into a more intimate relationship with our Bridegroom.

The psalmist referred to anointing as the "oil of gladness" (Ps. 45:7). Refraining from its use was a sign of mourning. It is possible, that because of Ruth's widowhood, she had refrained from anointing herself. Now she was being instructed to do so in preparation for presenting herself to her redeemer.

Put on Your Raiment

After washing and anointing herself, Naomi then instructed Ruth to take off her widow's garments that she had worked in, by which everyone knew her social status, and to put on her best raiment. The Scriptures speak allegorically of the significance of garments on other occasions. The prophet, Isaiah, in his messianic prophecy, speaks of God giving His people "the garment of praise for the spirit of heaviness" (Is. 61:3). The New Testament instructs us to "offer the sacrifice of praise to God continually, that is, the fruit of our lips giving thanks to his name" (Heb. 13:15). Taken together, these scriptures teach us that we are to come into the presence of our Kinsman-Redeemer clothed in a garment of praise and offering Him the fruit of our lips.

The Scriptures also teach us to put off the old man as though it were a garment. Paul declared:

> Set your affection on things above, not on things on the earth...Mortify therefore your members which are upon the earth; fornication, uncleanness, inordinate affection, evil concupiscence, and covetousness, which is idolatry...Lie not

one to another, seeing that ye have put off the old man with his deeds; And have put on the new man, which is renewed in knowledge after the image of him that created him (Col. 3:2,5,9-10).

Entering into complete commitment to Christ, our Redeemer, requires that we put off the old and put on the new. It is in choosing to make that commitment that we are given the divine ability to do so.

In many weddings in which I have officiated, it has been my privilege, as a woman, to go into the bride's dressing room. I watch the bridesmaids get ready first. Then everyone's eyes turn to the bride. The room is electric with the anticipation of the event that is at hand as I pray with her before the ceremony. She is always beautiful, and I tell her so, dressed in her lovely wedding gown. Brides don't wear mourning garments. They are dressed in once-in-a-lifetime elegance in anticipation of the happy event that is about to take place. It was in anticipation of Ruth's redemption that Naomi instructed Ruth to put off her widow's garment and put on her best raiment.

Go to the Threshing Floor

Having completed Naomi's instructions for preparation, Ruth was now ready to go to the threshing floor. What would she encounter there? There would most certainly be an atmosphere of festivity and joy because of the bountiful harvest that was filling the garners. And there would be the seemingly ceaseless activity of threshing of grain to preserve the harvest. All was done in the presence and under the watchful eye of Boaz.

These aspects of harvest — the festivity and joy, as well as the threshing, foreshadow the reality of praise and worship in the church today as the Holy Spirit is preparing her to come into the presence of her Redeemer. In the midst of our praise and rejoicing, however, there is also the cleansing work of winnowing and threshing, separating the chaff from the wheat, that is necessary for our preservation. John the Baptist declared of the coming of Jesus, "he shall baptize you with the Holy Ghost, and with fire: Whose fan is in his hand and he will thoroughly purge his floor, and gather his wheat into the garner; but he will burn up the chaff with unquenchable fire" (Matt. 3:11-12).

Ruth would not have found the rest she was seeking without going first to the threshing floor to ask for the covering of Boaz. Though it would be inaccurate to the allegory to say that Ruth herself experienced a winnowing process there, yet we can conclude that it was in the place where the chaff was separated from the wheat that the redeemer was to be found. Allegorically speaking, believers should expect to endure threshing floor experiences when the Lord Himself comes to separate the wheat from the chaff in our lives.

Faith, as well as obedience, is required for us to go to the threshing floor. As we have mentioned, it was the unbelief of the Israelites that kept them from receiving their inheritance in the promised land. As we have seen, they forfeited the rest God had promised them by refusing to believe God's Word to them. In contrast, it was Ruth's trust in God and her willing obedience to follow her mother-in-law's instructions that brought her safely to the place of redemption and, ultimately, into her promised rest. Obedience is always a result of faith, of believing the promises of God to the extent that we act on them. It is comforting to know that our faithful obedience, like Ruth's, will never go unrewarded.

Stand in the Shadows

Though there were undoubtedly other men at the threshing floor, Ruth was looking for only one. Boaz, her kinsman-redeemer was the only one of interest to her. She had been instructed to stand in the shadows, unnoticed, until the work was finished. When Boaz had eaten and drunk and had laid down for the night, Ruth was to find a place at his feet and lie quietly there, waiting for him to notice her.

These instructions may seem somewhat strange to us, perhaps even appearing to require improper conduct for one who was considered a virtuous woman. That is because we read our Western culture into the text. In virtue of an ancient and much prized Hebrew law, it was a custom for a woman to lie on the floor crosswise at the foot of a man that kinsman, to call upon him to fulfill his kinsman responsibilities.[3] No impropriety must be construed in our minds from this custom. For one who wanted to be redeemed, it was simply an accepted practice to lie at the feet of a redeemer in this manner.

Naomi had instructed Ruth to stay at the feet of Boaz until she got his attention. Then she could present her request to him and wait to hear what he would say to her. She had placed herself at his mercy, becoming vulnerable to his judgment. There was nothing to do now but to wait to see what this kinsman-redeemer would do for her.

Waiting: A Requirement

Waiting is a requirement for those who would enjoy the revelation of God's blessing. The psalmist declared:

> I waited patiently for the Lord; and he inclined unto me, and heard my cry. He brought me up also out of an horrible pit, out of the miry clay, and set my feet upon a rock, and established my goings (Ps. 40:1-2).

We cannot expect to know the blessings of relationship with God without spending time waiting upon Him. Even Jesus waited in prayer all night before His Father on several occasions. He commended Mary's willingness to sit at His feet, waiting to hear His words, while Martha complained that she had no help with the kitchen duties. When Martha asked Jesus to make Mary help her, He replied, "Martha, Martha, thou art careful and troubled about many things: But one thing is needful: and Mary hath chosen that good part, which shall not be taken away from her" (Luke 10:41-42).

Sitting at the Master's feet, listening to His words, Mary revealed her heart's desire for relationship with Him. Who we become in our relationship with Christ will be the result of our choice to wait on Him. We become worshipers, not by works, theology or human promotion, but by our own choice to wait before God, humbly listening for His voice. We must choose to go to the threshing floor and place ourselves at the feet of our Redeemer, asking for His covering.

Ruth, whose people were enemies of Israel, had come to Bethlehem-judah motivated by her deep desire to serve Naomi and Naomi's God. Now she had placed herself at the mercy of a wealthy Israelite, near kinsman to her mother-in-law. Would she be accepted as one of them in this place of redemption? That was her hope as she obeyed Naomi in all she instructed her to do. For now, all she could do was to wait for the response of Boaz. Boaz was a wealthy man, quite capable of fulfilling the role of kinsman-redeemer. He had both the power and the means to redeem Ruth. It remained yet to know if he would be willing to redeem her.

Boaz's Initial Response

That night when Boaz detected a woman lying

at his feet in the dark, he did not ask her what she wanted—he understood what she wanted. Rather his question to her was, "Who art thou?"

In simply saying her name, Ruth revealed the need of her life. All of the pathos of this beautiful love story is expressed in Ruth's tender plea: "I am Ruth thine handmaid: spread therefore thy skirt over thine handmaid." (Ruth 3:9).

In Eastern culture, to spread a skirt, or covering, over someone was a symbolic act offering that person protection. More than that, it involved entering into covenant with a person for the sake of redemption. Even today, in many Eastern countries to say that a man puts his skirt over a woman means that he marries her. The prophet Ezekiel gave us a beautiful picture of redemption, speaking to Israel as the voice of God: "Now when I passed by thee, and looked upon thee, behold, thy time was the time of love; and I spread my skirt over thee, and covered thy nakedness: yea, I sware unto thee, and entered into a covenant with thee, saith the Lord God, and thou becamest mine" (Ezek. 16:8).

In asking for Boaz to cover her, Ruth was declaring, "I need a redeemer. I am a widow, disgraced, with no inheritance. You can take my shame, my poverty, the bleakness of my future and give me an inheritance. You can totally redeem me, if you will."

In acknowledging the helplessness of her condition, Ruth typifies the helpless state of every person to redeem themselves. Only as we are willing to acknowledge our need of a Redeemer do we have hope of being delivered from our destitute, sinful state to receive the inheritance reserved for us in God. We ask for total redemption when we ask Christ to cover our sins with His blood. No one else can help us. If our Redeemer will not show us mercy, we will have to live without hope in our misery.

At the mention of her name, Boaz was reminded that this was the Moabitish widow who had come to care for her mother-in-law in this strange land and to serve the living God. Though she had won the admiration of the entire city because of her virtuous life (Ruth 3:11), she still desperately needed to be redeemed. For that reason she had come to this place to identify herself as one who was eligible for redemption.

In an earlier Bible story, Jacob, a desperate man who also needed redemption, found mercy when he identified himself to the angel with whom he wrestled. When the angel asked Jacob to tell him his name, Jacob whispered it, acknowledging its meaning — "cheater or supplanter." In that moment of painful revelation, the profound lack in his character was exposed to God. And together with that painful exposure came the redemption he so needed. As the angel touched Jacob's thigh, the strength of his nature was broken and his name was changed from *Jacob* to *Israel,* which means "prince of God."

Similarly, when Christians wait in the presence of their Redeemer, aware of their need of His redeeming power, they will receive revelation of their true nature in the light of His holiness. That carnal nature that wages war against our spirits will be exposed in the presence of God. As we confess who we are, He is able to change us, "spreading His skirt over us" as a covenant sign of our complete redemption. Not until we are willing to come to that place of reality in our Redeemer's presence can we expect to receive His favorable response.

The apostle Paul declared, "we all, with open face beholding as in a glass the glory of the Lord, are changed into the same image from glory to glory, even as by the Spirit of the Lord" (2 Cor. 3:18). As we choose to wait, open and vulnerable, in the presence of God, beholding Him in all His beauty, He will transform us by His Spirit into His image. This life-changing process, foreshadowed so beautifully by Ruth, prepares the church to enter into revelation of her Bridegroom and know the complete restoration promised her in Christ.

Ruth had already received the favor of Boaz, had eaten with him at his table and had been given handfuls on purpose. But to know the full redemption that Boaz was capable of giving her required this next step of going down to the threshing floor and waiting there in his presence.

Similarly, though believers experience salvation when they are born again, we understand from the Scriptures that our ultimate redemption requires a process of growth to bring us to maturity. It is then that we will reflect the character of Christ in our lives, being restored to the image of God. In order to enjoy this complete restoration, as believers we must cultivate a continual relationship of worship of our Redeemer. That relationship involves waiting in His presence and being willing to confess who we are as we see ourselves in the light of who He is.

Ruth's hopes for redemption were not to be disappointed. Boaz considered Ruth's offer of relationship a kindness to him. He blessed her for not going after young men, whether poor or rich. Then he gave her his reassurance that he would do all that was required for him to do. The deep admiration Boaz felt for Ruth was very apparent as he confirmed his willingness to restore her to her inheritance. His comforting words must have thrilled Ruth's heart as he reassured her of his intent to do all that was required.

There was a difficulty, however, in his redeeming her. Boaz informed Ruth that there was a another near kinsman who had first right of redemption of her. He would have to be confronted and dealt with according to the law of redemption. Boaz promised Ruth he would look into the matter on the morrow. Then he told Ruth to lie down until morning. What were the thoughts that raced through Ruth's mind as she lay there that night? Surely she could not have slept. She must have been filled with gratitude at her acceptance by Boaz. Excitement of her anticipated wedding day must have filled her heart. In the morning Boaz again showed the generosity of his redeemer-heart by giving Ruth six measures of barley to take home with her.

When Ruth returned home with the news of her encounter with Boaz, Naomi was delighted. She said to Ruth, "Sit still, my daughter, until thou know how the matter will fall: for the man will not be in rest, until he have finished the thing this day" (Ruth 3:18). Once again, Ruth was being required to wait. The matter was now out of their hands. They had placed it in the hands of their kinsman-redeemer. Yet, Ruth had already begun to enter into her rest simply by asking for it. There is a place of restful hope for us that we can find only after we have asked our Redeemer to "spread His skirt over us." Having confessed our need of redemption and waiting quietly in His presence, we can be sure that He will not delay in His response to us.

Only the matter of the nearer kinsman that must yet be resolved stood in the way of Ruth's wonderful restoration. As we understand who this kinsman foreshadows, we will understand the difficulty we encounter in securing our own redemption even after we have submitted ourselves to our lovely Redeemer. We, too, have a nearer kinsman that must be confronted before we can enjoy complete restoration.

9

Trial of the Kinsman

*R*uth's virtues have been seen in "all the city" (Ruth 3:11). Now her reward and recompense are to be as plainly apparent in the gates of the city. It is not Ruth, however, who claims our attention at the moment, it is Boaz. How will this kinsman-redeemer carry out his intent on her behalf? We have observed Boaz to be a man who is diligent in business, fervent in spirit, abundant in grace, ready to commend faithfulness in Ruth, generous, hospitable, wise and circumspect. These are all qualities every bride would dream of finding in a bridegroom. Our admiration for Boaz will inevitably deepen as we observe him fulfilling his role of kinsman-redeemer.

Sitting at the Gates

It is not only Boaz's moral character that commands great respect in the gates of the city but also his personal wealth and social rank. In these gates the inhabitants of the city were accustomed to gathering for business transactions, for hearing the news of the day and for conducting city meetings. The gates of these ancient cities served as guardhouses, markets, courts of justice and places for public deliberation and audience. Judges meted out justice to those who came for that purpose to the city gates. Even kings came to the gates to give audience to other kings and to their ambassadors as well.

The Scriptures refer allegorically to the "gates of the city" in other places. They hold great significance to Eastern culture. When we are instructed by the psalmist to "enter into his gates with thanksgiving" (Ps. 100:4), we understand that we are coming to the seat of divine justice to meet our King. As we come into the "city of God," to worship Him, our hearts should be filled with thanksgiving and praise for our King. He is our Protector and Provider of all that we need for life and happiness. As we worship Him in that place, we find an entrance into His presence that satisfies our hearts and meets the needs of our lives.

Boaz's Mission

Boaz arrived at the city gates that day for the sole purpose of doing what Ruth had asked of him. It was there that he would confront the nearer kinsman who had first right to her. Boaz was not an insensitive man, as we have observed. He knew well the regard that both Naomi and Ruth had for him. He was also deeply conscious that he was no longer responding impersonally to this beautiful girl from Moab who had come to trust under Jehovah's wing. His admiration for her had grown since that first day when he saw her gleaning in the field and had invited her to eat at his table. Now he was ready to challenge the nearer kinsman for the redemption of Elimelech's inheritance which included Ruth the Moabitess.

When Boaz encountered the nearer kinsman in the gate, he called him to a meeting with ten elders of the city, as the law required, to present the proposition of buying the inheritance of Elimelech. At first the nearer kinsman consented to redeem it. Then Boaz explained that in the day this kinsman redeemed the property of Elimelech, he also had to redeem Ruth, the Moabitess, "to raise up the name of the dead upon his inheritance" (Ruth 4:5). This the nearer kinsman refused to do, lest he mar his own inheritance (v. 6). He was not willing to marry this foreigner and ruin his bloodline for the sake of his posterity.

Who does this nearer kinsman represent allegorically? Who was this man who had first right to redeem Ruth? Boaz had told Ruth plainly that he was willing to redeem her. But legally, the claims of the nearer kinsman had to be resolved before Boaz had the right to redeem her.

Some Bible scholars feel that this nearer kinsman is a type of the world system, that many-faceted force that drives people to succeed. Many Christians are deceived through their own ambition into thinking that true satisfaction will come from a climb up society's corporate ladder. Should they reach their goal, they will come to the painful realization that the world system does not offer the rest or fulfillment they were seeking. There is no power of redemption in a world system where everyone is looking out for "number one" and resorting to manipulation and deception to secure their own interests. The greatest success the world system offers cannot compare to the rest for our souls that our Kinsman-Redeemer has provided for us.

Other scholars feel that this nearer kinsman is a type of the Law of Moses. Though the Law of Moses was given before the sacrifice of Calvary, representing God's standard of holiness for man, it was powerless to redeem mankind from sin. The Galatians were dangerously close to forfeiting their salvation because of placing their confidence in the observance of the Law instead of looking to Christ in faith for redemption. Paul exhorted them: "Wherefore the law was our schoolmaster to bring us unto Christ, that we might be justified by faith" (Gal. 3:24). The Law of Moses showed us right and wrong conduct, condemning our sinful behavior, but it could not give us the ability to overcome the power of sin. We are justified only by our faith in Christ who enables us to overcome sin in our lives.

It is sad to watch some Christians who have a fundamental misunderstanding of redemption, trying to live holy lives in their own strength. In their confusion, some try to redeem themselves, consciously or unconsciously, through doing good works — fulfilling an external code of righteousness. The Law of Moses requires good works, but it cannot give us the strength to do them. All it can do is condemn us for not living up to its standard. The Law serves only the purpose of bringing us to a consciousness of our need of a Redeemer. Though the Law of Moses had a valid place in the economy of God, it had no power to redeem mankind. Neither the world system nor the Law of Moses are able to provide the redemption mankind needs.

A third view of this nearer kinsman presents him as a type of every person's carnal nature or self-life, that which lies closer to each of us than either the world system or the Law of Moses. It is this carnal nature that defeats many Christians, keeping them from entering into their rest in God. The conflict between the old man and the new creation in Christ absorbed the apostle Paul's thinking as he wrote to the Romans, concluding that only Christ could deliver us from the wretchedness of our carnal nature (Rom. 7:25). Through His power alone are we able to overcome the power of sin, and "put on the new self, which in the likeness of God has been created in righteousness and holiness of the truth" (Eph. 4:24, NAS).

Contrary to what humanists and proponents of New Age philosophy teach, man is not basically good, and there is nothing within our own nature that chooses righteousness. According to the religion of humanism, each man is his own god, or redeemer. This atheistic philosophy is the fulfillment of the deception Satan used in the garden of Eden. He told Eve that if she disobeyed God's command not to eat of the tree of the knowledge of good and evil, "ye shall be as gods." It was that deception that caused the fall of the first Adam and his bride, and Satan will try again to deceive the bride of Christ with this philosophy based on self-realization apart from God. But our heavenly Bridegroom, the second Adam, will protect His bride from the deception of the evil one to bring us safely to Himself.

Humanism and New Age philosophies teach that through our power to choose we can realize our highest potential simply by making the right choices. This doctrine of self-realization is the highest form of selfishness found in humanity, creating a passionate self-centeredness that, as history has proved, will not promote the common good of anything or anyone. It is a deception to think, as humanists do, that all we will ever need to be successful and happy lies within us. That assumption is not only theologically incorrect, violating the doctrine of the total depravity of man, but is experientially unsound as well.

If we consider the history of man, observing the horrors of war alone shows us that the idea of man's innate goodness is fantasy. Even the humanists found it necessary to revise their *Humanist Manifesto,* first written in 1933, declaring it too optimistic.[1] During the forty years that followed the writing of that atheistic treatise, mankind endured two world wars and other bloody conflicts around the world. The *Humanist Manifesto* declares: "The goal of humanism is a free and universal society in which people voluntarily and intelligently cooperate for the common good.

Man is at last becoming aware that he alone is responsible for the realization of the world of his dreams, that he has within himself the power for its achievement."[2] To say that people will make benevolent, unselfish, choices that will redeem mankind to its highest potential in the face of such tragic historical evidence is nothing short of insanity. All of history concurs that the carnal nature of man inevitably leads to moral destruction without the intervention of our Kinsman-Redeemer, Jesus Christ.

In the book of Ruth, we have observed how dramatically our God-given power of choice can affect our lives. As we choose to give our lives to God, He enables us to make right decisions for our lives according to His eternal plan for them. However, apart from God there is no redemptive power in human choices. If left to our own choices, our self-life, while promising us the best of everything, only produces death. In Proverbs we read, "There is a way which seemeth right unto a man, but the end thereof are the ways of death" (Prov. 14:12).

Having observed three possibilities for the

identity of the nearer kinsman, we can see that all three represent a formidable foe to the true Redeemer. Whether we conclude that, in type, Ruth's nearer kinsman foreshadows the world system, the Law of Moses or our carnal nature, it is clear that he stands for everything that says no to God's redemptive will for our lives. In reality, to the degree that any of these three nearer-kinsmen influence our lives, we need to ask our Kinsman-Redeemer to challenge them and buy us back from their destructive influence.

It is interesting to note that although Ruth's nearer kinsman was concerned for his own posterity in not redeeming her, his name is dropped forever from the annals of history. Though Boaz would certainly have called him by name, the historian did not record it for us. His posterity has fallen into complete obscurity, while the name of Boaz will be remembered forever.

Christ, our *Goel*, challenged these nearer-kinsmen as He was crucified outside the city gates between two thieves. He lived in the world as One who did only the will of His Father, never seeking His own will. He fulfilled all the requirements of the Law of Moses and lived a sinless life. Through His obedience, Jesus challenged the rights of these nearer kinsmen to redeem us. Though it was necessary for the Redeemer of mankind to fulfill the Law of Moses and to live a sinless life, that alone could not secure our redemption.

For the redemption of mankind to be realized, there needed to be a reordering of authority for three elements — law, grace and flesh. The Law had to yield to grace in the blood atonement Jesus made. And flesh simply had to be crucified. It would not have been necessary for Jesus to lay down His life if simply living in perfect obedience to the Law of Moses could have redeemed us. As our heavenly *Goel*, He carried both the Law and our sinful self-life outside the city gate to make the priceless exchange at Calvary for our redemption.

Christ bore the reproach of dying in disgrace to buy back everything mankind had lost since the fall of Adam. In that supreme sacrifice, He robbed the other kinsmen of their rights and restored to us the possibility of relationship with the living God as He had intended it from the beginning. Jesus said, "I am the good shepherd: the good shepherd giveth his life for the sheep...No man taketh it from me, but I lay it down of myself" (John 10:11,18). The love of Boaz for this Moabitish woman foreshadows the fulfillment for all mankind of the love of Christ that caused Him to lay down His life to redeem us.

Sealing the Covenant

Now this was the manner in former time in Israel concerning redeeming and concerning changing, for to confirm all things; a man plucked off his shoe, and gave it to his neighbour: and this was a testimony in Israel (Ruth 4:7).

After the nearer kinsman had renounced his right to redeem Elimelech's property, he took off his shoe and gave it to Boaz. This custom originated with the ancient practice of taking possession of fixed property by treading upon the soil. After the death of Moses, when the Lord spoke to Joshua to take the people into the land of Canaan, He promised that, "Every place that the sole of your foot shall tread upon, that have I given unto you, as I said unto Moses" (Josh. 1:3). This literal walking into the land gave possession of their inheritance to the Israelites. God Himself went with them to fight their enemies and give them victory.

In later times, this act of taking off the shoe and handing it to the person to whom property was being transferred was a sign of the sealing of a covenant. It became a symbol of the transfer of a possession or right of ownership. Boaz was figuratively treading upon everything that the nearer kinsman had any rights to redeem, sealing the fact that everything Ruth needed had been purchased for her by her kinsman-redeemer.

This custom is a picture of the eternal redemption wrought for us by Christ. In the first prophetic glimpse of redemption found in the Scriptures, God declared to the serpent, "And I will put enmity between thee and the woman, and between thy seed and her seed; it shall bruise thy head, and thou shalt bruise his heel" (Gen. 3:15). The Scriptures teach that Jesus' heel bruised the head of Satan when He redeemed everything that the devil had stolen from man. Prophetically, the seed of the woman was Jesus, who bruised Satan's head at

Calvary, buying back our rightful inheritance in God.

In bruising the head of Satan, Jesus fulfilled the eternal plan of redemption so that it would be possible for us to live in victory over all our enemies. The Scriptures declare, "For this purpose the Son of God was manifested, that he might destroy the works of the devil" (1 John 3:8). Here the word *destroy* means to undo, outdo and overdo everything the devil ever did. Jesus will undo for us everything that needs to be undone so that we can fulfill our divine destiny in God.

Witnesses to the Deed

Upon the completion of the transaction of Ruth's redemption, Boaz turned to the elders and all the people standing there and said to them, "You are witnesses today that I have bought from the hand of Naomi all that belonged to Elimelech and all that belonged to Chilion and Mahlon" (Ruth 4:9, NAS). They responded, "We are witnesses." Then they blessed Ruth.

The church stands as a witness today that Christ has sealed the covenant of our redemption. We who are redeemed rejoice each time another comes to the place of redemption to receive his or her inheritance. Jesus did not make a conditional promise for just a few to enter this inheritance. He will not deny this blessing to anyone who truly seeks rest in Him. Our Redeemer went outside the city gates, gave Himself for a ransom, bought us with His own blood and redeemed our forfeited inheritances. He has taken all of us who come to Him unto Himself to protect us and make us His bride (see 1 Pet. 1:18-19; Heb. 9:12-15).

Everything that challenges our redemption has been dealt with at Calvary. That is why we must continually live at the cross in order to realize the wonderful redemption that Christ has won for us. Jesus said we must take up our cross daily to follow Him (Luke 9:23). And the apostle Paul declared, "I die daily" (1 Cor. 15:31). Release from our sin and carnal self-life was made possible by the sacrifice of Calvary. It remains for us to choose to die to all that would hinder our redemption.

The power of the Holy Spirit enables us to choose God's will. As we make those choices, we will enter into intimate relationship with our Bridegroom. He will transform us and cause us to triumph in all of life. The beautiful transformation of Ruth's life is but a foreshadowing of the resurrection life that Christ gives to all who come to Him.❦

10

Triumph and Transformation

*T*he wonder of redemption is that it restores us to a place of greater blessing than we enjoyed before our unfortunate loss. When Christ, our Kinsman-Redeemer, comes to buy back everything we have lost, the quality of divine life He gives us thrusts us into a greater dimension of eternal worth than we have ever known before. Perhaps this seems incomprehensible. Perhaps the terrible suffering and loss we have endured makes such restoration seem impossible.

How could Naomi be restored to her husband or her two sons? No one could bring them back to her. Naomi's loss seems unredeemable, as does Ruth's loss of her husband. Many Christians live in despair today because they view their sorrows in this way — irreversible, unredeemable. They have not understood the principle of divine restoration.

Can you imagine Naomi's joy as she helped Ruth prepare for her wedding as the bride of Boaz? It would have been natural for Naomi and Ruth to reminisce concerning the heart decisions that had brought her to this glorious event. Could these two widows have anticipated such a wonderful occasion as this a few months earlier as they prepared to leave Moab, turning back to the House of Bread? Though their hearts had been severely tested, they had placed their trust in Jehovah, and He was proving His faithfulness to them.

Naomi and Ruth had left Moab, a land of idolatry, and positioned themselves for redemption through obedience and commitment to the living God. Now, not only was Ruth serving God in the House of Bread but she was also to become the wife of a wealthy lord of the land. She had already begun to experience divine blessings on a life she had never known before.

And soon, through the blessing of God, she would bear her husband a son. The Scriptures declare, "So Boaz took Ruth, and she was his wife: and when he went in unto her, the Lord gave her conception, and she bare a son" (Ruth 4:13). Ruth had not known the joy of motherhood until now. As a result of her redemption, Ruth experienced greater fulfillment as a woman than she had known before. The Lord had removed her barrenness and had given her a son.

Naomi was also enjoying the blessing of her personal restoration. Her neighbors said to Naomi, "Blessed be the Lord, which hath not left thee this day without a kinsman, that his name may be famous in Israel. And he shall be unto thee a restorer of thy life, and a nourisher of thine old age: for thy daughter-in-law, which loveth thee, which is better to thee than seven sons, hath borne him" (Ruth 4:14-15). These women named the child Obed, which means "the serving one," perhaps prophetically anticipating the way he would serve his grandmother in her old age.

What a transformation of Naomi's and Ruth's lives from the forlorn women they were as they returned to the House of Bread! What exciting dimensions their lives entered into as they began to assume the duties for their wealthy household and the rearing of this precious son! Yet as wonderful as these relationships seem, the greater wonder of the restoration of Naomi and of Ruth is the eternal significance of their redemption. It eclipses the wonder of these precious temporal blessings.

It is the genealogy of this son that reveals the eternal aspect of their restoration. According to the genealogy given here, Ruth's baby son, Obed, would one day become the father of Jesse, who would become the father of King David, ruler of

Israel. Ruth's obedience to God filled her life with wonderful temporal blessings. But of far greater significance, her posterity became part of a royal lineage. It is interesting to note that although the near kinsman feared he would mar his posterity by marrying Ruth, in reality, Ruth's redemption placed her posterity in a line of royalty.

Perhaps we cannot appreciate the greater wonder of Ruth's true restoration because the importance of posterity has largely been lost to our American culture. However, for a Moabitish woman to be transferred into relationship with a wealthy lord of Israel whose seed would be a part of such a line of royalty was a wonder even to the Jews who wrote the genealogies. The genealogy given here closes with David, an evident proof that the book of Ruth was intended to give a family picture from the life of the pious ancestors of this great and godly king of Israel.

If we cannot comprehend the significance of Ruth's restoration so far, how can we fully appreciate the greater significance of her posterity as revealed to us in the New Testament? All the members of the genealogy of David whose names occur here are also found in the New Testament genealogy of Jesus Christ. "The passage is given by Matthew word for word in the genealogy of Christ, that we may see that this history looks not so much to David as to Jesus Christ, who was proclaimed by all as the Savior and Redeemer of the human race, and that we may learn with what wonderful compassion the Lord raises up the lowly and despised to the greatest glory and majesty."[1]

Through her obedience to God first, and then to Naomi, Ruth realized her personal restoration as a wife and mother with honor and security and deep womanly satisfaction. But of far greater significance, in the mercy of God, this stranger to Israel also became a significant part of the genealogy of our Lord Jesus Christ. Her marriage to Boaz had placed her in the royal lineage of the One who came to save mankind. Every Jewish woman in Israel, it seems, should have been more eligible for this honor than Ruth, the Moabitess. Yet, it pleased God to grant it to her.

What precious hope this historical reality gives the church today! Though we were strangers and aliens to God, He has redeemed us unto Himself without regard for our past or our questionable "bloodline." And as we follow Him in obedience, we will receive revelation of Him and be transformed into His image, becoming the bride of Christ. Out of our intimate love relationship with our Bridegroom, we will reflect the character of the King of kings in our lives and will one day reign with Him eternally.

The redemption Boaz promised to Ruth was indeed clearly and openly manifested in the sight of all. Her restoration foreshadows the reality of the New Testament command to all to "Humble yourselves therefore under the mighty hand of God, that he may exalt you in due time" (1 Pet. 5:6). Ruth chose to follow the God of her mother-in-law, just as the wise men followed the star that appeared in the east, not knowing where they were going but trusting as they went. The wise men were not disappointed as they worshiped their Redeemer.

Neither was Ruth disappointed as she found her kinsman-redeemer. Faith had sustained her as, in total commitment, she left all behind saying, "Thy people shall be my people, and thy God my God" (Ruth 2:16). She had been willing to become a lonely gleaner toiling under the hot sun, probably gossiped about by the women of the city as "that Moabitish woman" who had come with Naomi. Following Naomi's instructions, she unashamedly sought for a covering, pleading, "spread therefore thy skirt over thine handmaid; for thou art a near kinsman" (Ruth 3:9). Her claims for justice were not disdained, for there was one in Israel who had marked her faithfulness and virtue.

Boaz had seen her walk, her talk and her heart's desire — not only in the harvest fields, but during that difficult and delicate time when she waited at the threshing floor. The heart of Boaz had been moved to shelter her under the spreading wings of his own name and inheritance. Desolate though she had been, he purchased her for himself before all the assembled company to bring forth a heritage through her.

The Lord's blessing was upon their marriage as seen in the birth of Obed. His birth foreshadows the life of Christ being reproduced in the church. As the church matures in the revelation of Christ, she will bring forth sons and daughters for posterity. As Boaz, a type of Christ, reproduced his life through Obed for posterity, so Christ desires to reproduce His life in us, to show forth His character for eternity.

The people prayed for Ruth to "do thou worthily in Ephratah, and be famous in Bethlehem" (Ruth 4:11). The name Ephratah means "fruitful." Doing worthily in Ephratah signifies begetting and training worthy sons and daughters who will make her name renowned. That is the calling of the church as well. Not only will Christ bring us into divine rest ourselves, forming His character in us, but He will also cause us to bring forth fruit in His kingdom — sons and daughters who will love God.

Christ is the Restorer of all that was lost in the fall of mankind in the garden of Eden. He is the Lamb, slain from the foundation of the world — before flesh ever fell and Law ever came. He stands today as our *Goel* — Redeemer. He came to destroy the works of the evil one and to establish His church in the earth as a testimony to His great redemption. Through the victory of Calvary, He is able to save us to the uttermost. One day He will present to the Father a glorious church without spot or wrinkle. As His spotless bride, we will reign with Him in His kingdom forever.

An Eternal Kingdom

This wonderful eternal aspect of Christ's kingdom is foreshadowed in the people's prophetic words to Ruth: "The Lord make the woman that is come into thine house like Rachel and like Leah, which two did build the house of Israel" (Ruth 4:11). The whole nation of Israel came from Rachel and Leah. Though other great empires have come and gone, Israel is a nation today. Babylon is gone. The glory of Greece is gone. The Roman Empire is gone, and every kingdom that has ever raised its head to say that they were mightier than the living God has crumbled and disappeared. But the children of Rachel and Leah are still living today in fulfillment of prophecy.

In that same way, the church has survived terrible satanic onslaughts throughout history and will continue to gain in strength, while every enemy that has exalted itself against her falls and will be remembered no more. Only the church is eternal, proving its superiority over every philosophy, false religion and other empires that would challenge her.

In Boaz, Ruth not only found the purchaser of property for her but she found her bridegroom, who gave her rest and through whom she conceived new life, placing her in the lineage of Christ. Ruth's restoration foreshadows the wonderful hope for the church which, in the end, will have restored to her everything that Jesus bought for her at Calvary. A new day is dawning for the church. The day of her restoration is at hand. Revival is coming to the land. To enter into this new day, we need to heed the word that God is visiting His people with fresh bread and turn our hearts from our personal Moab to go to the House of Bread. There we will begin to see the process of redemption fulfilled in our lives as our "hap happens" to bring us to the field of our Kinsman-Redeemer.

We all have choices to make in order to enter

into the kind of relationship with our Lord that will culminate in our complete redemption. In that redemption we will be restored to a better inheritance than we knew before we experienced the tragedy of famine in our lives. Faith, humility and obedience will be required as we follow the wise counsel of the Scriptures and of those "Naomis" to whose spiritual authority we are accountable in the Lord.

There is a rest prepared for the people of God that the church has not yet entered. All that is foreshadowed in the book of Ruth can be ours if we choose to let nothing keep us from following after our God. We can trust the great redeemer-heart of Christ, our heavenly Goel, to do all that is required for our redemption. As we yield to the preparation processes that will take us ultimately to the threshing floor, let us humbly ask Him to spread His cover over us.

In that place of worship at Jesus' feet, we will begin to enter into the eternal rest that He has purchased for us. It won't be long before He will consummate the relationship, creating fruitfulness in our lives and placing us into His eternal, royal lineage.

Christ, our Redeemer, is sufficient and able as King of kings to do all that we ask. He has redeemed us and is continually redeeming us. Having completed our obedience, let us "sit still and see how the matter will fall" (Ruth 3:18). As we wait on the Lord for complete restoration, we can rejoice with Jude in this wonderful promise:

Now unto him that is able to keep you from falling, and to present you faultless before the presence of his glory with exceeding joy, To the only wise God our Saviour, be glory and majesty, dominion and power, both now and ever. Amen (Jude 24-25). ♥

11

This Present Light

Have we grasped the magnitude and wonder of God's plan for restoration for our individual lives and for His church as it is foreshadowed prophetically in the book of Ruth? Or, do our minds defeat us with thoughts of, "It's too good to be true" or "Maybe someday, but surely not now." Can we really hope to be a part of a church "without spot or wrinkle" in our day?

Arise, shine; for thy light is come, and

the glory of the Lord is risen upon thee. For, behold, the darkness shall cover the earth, and gross darkness the people: but the Lord shall arise upon thee, and his glory shall be seen upon thee (Is. 60:1-2).

Many have become disheartened and tempted to lose their hope as they view their personal walk with God candidly, as well as looking around at others and to the church in general. Others have at least been tempted to push this wonderful truth of revival and restoration into a future time, not expecting it to be fulfilled for them personally. They do not expect to experience such dramatic transformation from their present condition to the divine restoration that Naomi and Ruth enjoyed.

The prophet Isaiah declared, "Arise, shine; for thy light is come, and the glory of the Lord is risen upon thee" (Is. 60:1). In a time when darkness covers the earth and gross darkness the people, Isaiah said that the glory of the Lord is risen upon His people. Surely, if we look around us to witness the iniquity of our land, we must conclude that our society today qualifies as a time when darkness covers the earth. The church has reeled under the impact of the sin that runs rampant in our nation. Yet, it is in such a time of terrible spiritual darkness that the prophet dares to declare, "Arise, shine; for thy light is come and the glory of the Lord is risen upon thee." It is significant that the prophet's exhortation to arise was written emphatically in the present tense.

"I AM"

Our Lord Jesus Christ does not relate to mankind in the past tense or in the future tense. Though we refer to the life He lived on the earth in past tense, and look with anticipation to His second coming in future tense, Christ does not acknowledge our time limitations of past or future. He outraged the Jews on one occasion by declaring to them, "Before Abraham was, I am" (John 8:58).

While we may not have a problem accepting intellectually the eternalness of Christ, I think we still have a tendency in reality to relate to Him in the past and future rather than in the present. We read in the Scriptures of His wonderful deeds in the past and live with the hope of His coming in the future. But who is Christ in the reality of our lives today?

Jesus declared, "I am the way, the truth, and the life: no man cometh unto the Father, but by me" (John 14:6). He said also, "I am the living bread which came down from heaven: if any man eat of this bread, he shall live for ever" (John 6:51). To Martha, who was grieving over the death of her brother, Lazarus, Jesus declared, "I am the resurrection, and the life" (John 11:25). On other occasions Jesus taught His disciples, declaring, "I am the door" (John 10:9), "I am the good shepherd" (John 10:11), "I am the light of the world" (John 8:12). To John the Revelator, on the isle of Patmos, He declared, "I am Alpha and Omega, the beginning and the end. I will give unto him that is athirst of the fountain of the water of life freely" (Rev. 21:6).

It is the "I AM" of Christ, the present tense reality of His person, who we must know as our *Goel*-Redeemer for the needs of our lives today. That is where Ruth encountered Boaz as she made known her present needs to him. Only in that way can we, as did Ruth, enter into the rest God has promised us.

As a pastor, I have counseled many people who have said, "You don't understand what I need." That may be true, but Christ does understand. If we say, "I need grace," He responds, "I AM." Or, "I need peace in my home," He declares, "I AM the Prince of Peace." We should not blame Him for the needs we have when we are not allowing Him to be the I AM He has promised to be for those needs. We must learn to respond to Him in the present tense, through faith, allowing Him to be the I AM for all our needs. Then we will experience the transformation of our lives as His glory rests upon us.

His Glory

What is the glory of the Lord? Believers have long cried out for the Lord to send the glory. What is it we are looking for? What do we call the glory? Where is it coming from? I have been guilty of thinking that the glory would be something like a cloud that was seen in the wilderness covering the people of Israel or a pillar of fire coming to settle on our churches — some special manifestation of the presence of God.

When I was pastoring Fountain Gate Ministries, the church I founded in Dallas, Texas, I had an unfortunate experience with a minister whom I trusted. He came to our church and told me that the glory would not come to our church. He said because our church was in America, and because I was a woman pastor, we would not see the glory of God. I was grieved for several weeks because I trusted this minister as a man of God who had done a great work in another country. I even tried to make another male minister the titular head of my church so that I would not hinder the glory of God coming to our church. However, the Lord spoke firmly to me to "stand in the podium and allow the oil of the Spirit to take the shape of the vessel through whom it was poured." As a woman, God had called me to be a pastor, and all I needed was the anointing of the Holy Spirit to be poured through me.

I continued to cry out for the Lord to send His glory to our church. Early one Sunday morning I was walking back and forth before the altar of our church crying out, "Oh, Lord, send Your glory. Let Your glory come down."

With that cry still on my lips, I heard the Holy Spirit ask me, "Fuchsia, what are you looking for?"

"The glory," I said.

"What shape will it be?" He asked me. "A funnel? A balloon? A cloud? What color will it be? Silver, blue, pink?" I knew then that He was being facetious, pointing out my wrong concept of "the glory." However, He did not say anymore to me about the glory, though I continued praying about it.

Three weeks later, during a Sunday morning worship service, I was standing on the platform with my eyes closed and my hands raised, worshiping the Lord. I felt the Holy Spirit tell me to open my eyes. One-third of my congregation was young people, and my immediate thought was that perhaps one of them was misbehaving. I opened my eyes and looked around the congregation. Everyone was standing and worshiping the Lord, enjoying His presence.

So I closed my eyes again and continued to worship. The Holy Spirit seemed to punch me again and tell me to open my eyes. I asked Him, "What am I supposed to be looking for?"

"Look at your people," He said.

In that moment, scales came off my spiritual eyes, and I said to Him, "I see lit front porch lights on all the faces of these people. The glory of the Lord is shining through their countenances. He is at home in my people."

I understood then that it was not correct to ask, "*What* is the glory?" but rather to ask, "*Who* is the glory?" The Scriptures declare that Jesus is the "brightness of his glory, and the express image of his person" (Heb. 1:3), revealing the Father to us. It is the manifested presence of Christ shining forth through His people that is the glory of God in the earth. He expects to do that in the present — now — in the lives of His people that He is redeeming.

Present Glory

Every temple God built throughout the history of His people has been a type of the living temples that Christians are to become in reality. The apostle Paul declared, "Know ye not that ye are the temple of God, and that the Spirit of God dwelleth in you?" (1 Cor. 3:16). When we study the history of God's people, we learn that God never built a temple that He did not fill with His glory.

Where will the glory come from and what will it look like? The glory of God that fills our temples is simply the manifestation of the resurrection life of Jesus living in believers. The apostle Paul referred to this fact when he wrote, "Christ in you, the hope of glory" (Col. 1:27). Why do we not see more glory shining through believers' lives? It is one thing for Christians to give mental assent to those words; it is quite another to choose to allow Christ to live His life through us and fill us with His presence.

Releasing the Glory

Considering the analogy of the temple, we remember that the tabernacle of Moses, built according to the pattern given by God on the mount, had three separate compartments — the outer court, the holy place and the holy of holies. God's presence dwelt in the holy of holies. Only one man, the high priest, could enter this place one day a year to make atonement for the nation.

In David's tabernacle, these separations were disregarded, as David reached prophetically into the reality of grace as it was to be fulfilled in Christ. David assigned hundreds of people to offer sacrifices and praise continually before the presence of the ark. Because of grace, we can all experience the presence of God as often as we desire. In Solomon's temple, however, the glory of God filled it so entirely that the priests could not stand to minister. God's manifest presence there eclipsed the earlier manifestations of Himself to His people.

Today, God is building His church in believers' lives, temples not made with hands. As human temples of God, we are destined to manifest His glory in the earth today. We sometimes refer to man as a tripartite being, consisting of body, soul and spirit. Though that is a correct description of fallen man, that is not what God created man to be. In the same way that God did not originally intend to limit His presence to the holy of holies in the tabernacle of Moses, He does not intend for us to limit His presence in our lives to our spirits, our inner man, while our souls — our minds, wills and emotions — live independently of His presence. It is this separation that keeps us from manifesting the glory of God in our lives.

God's plan was to pour Himself into mankind through communion with him. When He walked through the garden after Adam and Eve had hidden in fear because of their disobedience, God's cry must have been filled with pathos and grief as He called out, "Adam, where are you?" When mankind sinned, a veil was dropped between his spirit and his soul as surely as there was a curtain separating the holy of holies from the holy place in the tabernacle of Moses. Since that time, every person has been separated from God, his or her spirit dead to God. The Scriptures declare we were dead in trespasses and sins (Eph. 2:1).

When we are born again, the Holy Spirit deposits the same "incorruptible seed" in our spirits that He deposited in the uterus of Mary. The life of Jesus is created in us. The Holy Spirit said to Mary, "That holy thing which shall be born of thee shall be called the Son of God" (Luke 1:35). This is what Paul called, "Christ in you, the hope of glory" (Col. 1:27).

Although Christ is alive in our spirits after we are born again, our souls are still fallen under the bondage of sin. When the veil dropped between the spirit and soul of mankind, our wills became rebellious, our minds became a carnal enemy of God and our emotions became expressions of our rebellion. When Jesus came into our spirits and we were born again, He loosed our spirits and brought life to a third part of our being. Then He began to work by His Spirit to break the chains of sin off our minds, our wills and our emotions to cleanse us of our independence and rebellion. The Holy Spirit showed me that we cannot go to heaven without this work. He said, "I kicked independence and rebellion out of heaven one time with Lucifer, and I will not let it back in."

To manifest His glory in our temples, God sets a process in motion that we might call surgery. The

Scriptures refer to this divine surgery when they declare:

> For the word of God is quick, and powerful, and sharper than any twoedged sword, piercing even to the dividing asunder of soul and spirit, and of the joints and marrow, and is a discerner of the thoughts and intents of the heart (Heb. 4:12).

The Holy Spirit does not do this work instantly, but gradually. As we yield to Him, He severs the veil between our soul and spirit and allows the manifested presence of Christ to shine forth in our lives. Though Christ has been locked up in the church behind veils of flesh, our Teacher, the precious Holy Spirit, has come to rend those veils in believers' lives so that the light of God can shine forth through His church.

The Prodigal Is Coming Home

For the church to be filled with the glory of God, she must be willing to return to the place of God's blessing. We must choose, as Naomi and Ruth chose, to place ourselves in the place of blessing so that God can bring His wonderful revival and restoration to our lives. In the present renewal or visitation that the church is experiencing, prodigals are beginning to turn from their personal Moabs and return home.

Naomi, who represents the church age, was a

prodigal who had lived in the presence of God and had left because of famine in the land. But at the news of fresh visitation from God, she returned to Bethlehem-judah, to the living God, bringing Ruth with her. The Holy Spirit spoke to me regarding the prodigal church today, saying, "The seed of God is incorruptible, it cannot be killed. When I have planted it, no faulty church program is going to destroy it." Although much of the church today is under the bondage of "judges" ruling the land, and every man is doing what is right in his own eyes, God is having mercy and visiting His people again. He will bring restoration to His church today in the same way He did for Ruth so long ago.

I had not understood, as I taught the restoration of Ruth, that the restoration of Naomi was happening at the same time. I rejoiced in the fact that Ruth found grace in the eyes of Boaz, that he covered her with his mantle and chose her to be his bride as she sanctified herself to come into his presence. I saw the pattern for revival in that allegory, but then I reached the part of the allegory where Obed was born to Boaz and Ruth and laid into the lap of Naomi. This new life, coming forth from the divine union of Boaz and Ruth, represents the life of Christ coming forth in the church. As this baby was laid in the lap of Naomi, so the life of Christ is to be presented to the "prodigal" church. Her restoration is included in the plan of redemption. I suddenly understood that everyone who chooses to come back to the House of Bread, to the presence of God, can experience personal restoration and have the life of Jesus fill their lives.

Many Christians in denominational churches that turned from the presence of God in favor of tradition, form and ritual are beginning to turn once again to worship the living God. They are receiving the fresh visitation that God is bringing to the church. They will experience the grace of restoration in their lives and churches as they choose to seek the presence of the living God, their *Goel*-Redeemer. As the prodigal church seeks God during this evil time when darkness covers the earth, her light will shine as the glory of God is risen upon her.

When that happens, the prophet declared, "Gentiles shall come to thy light, and kings to the brightness of thy rising" (Is. 60:3). For these promises to be fulfilled, there must be a revival of the church as we have never known. I believe it has already begun. As the church continues to allow the processes of the Holy Spirit as demonstrated in the life of Ruth to cleanse and prepare her, she will know eternal restoration and find her rest in the presence of her Bridegroom.

Only do not let us miss this present light by relegating Christ to a historical or future reality. In our individual lives, as well as corporately in our churches, we must learn to yield to the I AM of resurrection life and power. Then we will obey the exhortation of the prophet to "Arise, shine; for thy light is come, and the glory of the Lord is risen upon thee" (Is. 60:1). The revival described by Isaiah in the verses following that declaration is of such vast proportions that we can hardly grasp the wonder of it. I believe it is for the church today!

I desire to be a part of this coming revival with all my heart. Anyone who desires to experience what God is doing in the earth today, and is willing to pay the price to let the glory of God shine through their lives, will not be disappointed. They will discover that their *Goel*-Redeemer will do greater works of restoration and redemption in their lives than they could have imagined possible! And the church is going to be restored to the inheritance that Christ died to give her! She will become a glorious church, without spot or wrinkle!

May we as individuals and as the church of Jesus Christ not settle for anything less than entering into our eternal rest in God, which is our divine inheritance. As we continually surrender our lives to God, we are being restored to the eternal purposes of God for His bride in the earth, fulfilling our eternal destiny, as we have seen foreshadowed so beautifully in the life of Ruth.

Notes

Chapter One
"HIStory" of Redemption

1.   Fuchsia Pickett, *For Such a Time as This* (Shippensburg, Pa.: Destiny Image, 1992), pp. 3-6.
2.   Ibid.

Chapter Three
Famine's Tragedy — A Cry for Redemption

1.   Reference from a course called "Becoming Who You Are," by Dutch Sheets, senior pastor of Spring Harvest Fellowship, Colorado Springs, Colorado, and adjunct professor for Christian Life School of Theology.
2.   David Jeremiah, *Invasion of Other Gods* (Dallas, Tex.: Word Publishing, 1995), pp. 29, 33-34.
3.   Fuchsia Pickett, *The Next Move of God* (Lake Mary, Fla.: Creation House, 1994), p. 13.

Chapter Four
The Turning of Naomi

1.   For a more complete testimony of Dr. Pickett's healing, read: Fuchsia Pickett, *God's Dream* (Shippensburg, Pa.: Destiny Image, 1995), pp. 44-49.

Chapter Seven
The Treatment of Ruth

1.   Keil-Delitzsch, *Commentary on the Old Testament,* vol. 2 (Grand Rapids, Mich.: Eerdmans, 1975), p. 480.
2.   Douglas, J.D., et al., *New Bible Dictionary,* 2nd ed. (Wheaton, Ill.: Tyndale House Publishers, 1987), p. 745.

Chapter Eight
Tarrying for the Appointment

1.   Keil-Delitzsch, *Commentary on the Old Testament,* vol. 2 (Grand Rapids, Mich.: Eerdmans, 1975), p. 484.

2.   To obtain a copy of Dr. Pickett's study guide on the anointing, write to: Fuchsia Pickett, The Anointing, 394 Glory Road, Blountville, TN 37617.

3.   H.D.M. Spence and Joseph S. Exell, eds., *Pulpit Commentary,* vol. 4 (Grand Rapids, Mich.: Eerdmans, 1950), p. 48.

Chapter Nine
Trial of the Kinsman

1.   *Humanist Manifestos I and II,* ed. Paul Kurtz (Buffalo, N.Y.: Prometheus Books, 1973), p. 13.

2.   Ibid., p. 10.

Chapter Ten
Triumph and Transformation

1.   Keil-Delitzsch, *Commentary on the Old Testament,* vol. 2 (Grand Rapids, Mich.: Eerdmans, 1975), pp. 493-494.

About the Author

A native of Virginia, Dr. Pickett was raised in North Carolina. Answering the Lord's call to minister the Word of God, she studied at John Wesley College and Virginia Bible College. She has an earned doctorate in the field of theology as well as a doctorate of divinity. She is an ordained minister. She has taught in Bible colleges for more than forty years, and pastored for twenty-seven years.

In 1959, Dr. Pickett became seriously ill with a

life-threatening disease. On April 12, 1959, she was carried into a church service where God miraculously changed the course of her life. She was healed from the disease and baptized in the Holy Spirit. She declares that the greatest thing that ever happened to her occurred when her Teacher came in the Person of the Holy Spirit to establish a live-in relationship with her.

Dr. Pickett ministered as a conference evangelist and teacher during the next seven years. In 1966 she moved to Texas where she became affiliated with a large Bible college and served as head of its Bible department as academic dean and, subsequently, as director of the college.

Dr. Pickett and her husband, Leroy, founded Fountain Gate Ministries in 1971. This ministry included an interdenominational church, preschool, academy and college as well as a nationwide tape lending library, video extension program, daily radio program and weekly television ministry.

Since 1988 Dr. Pickett has traveled extensively and is in great demand as a conference speaker, gifted teacher and author, preparing and encouraging leaders to bring the church into her inheritance. She and her husband are based at Shekinah Ministries in Blountville, Tennessee.

Other Books by Fuchsia Pickett

For Such a Time as This
Price: $7

The life of Queen Esther bears greater significance for us than simply her reign as an historical queen. To fulfill His purposes on earth, God must have sons and daughters who determine to respond to the piercing question: Who knows whether you have been brought to the kingdom for such a time as this?

God's Dream
Price: $8

This book takes us into the heart of God, gives us insight into the Father's dream and reveals the sense of purpose that has motivated everything He has done, is doing and will do before time ceases to be. You will find the answers to the innate questions of every human heart.

Presenting the Holy Spirit (Volume 1)
Price: $11

Speaking from personal and ministerial experience, Dr. Pickett describes the unforgettable impact the vibrant person of the Holy Spirit makes on human lives and destinies.

Presenting the Holy Spirit (Volume 2)
Price: $13.95

This second volume presents the work of the Holy Spirit in the individual believer and in the church. Only as we learn to allow the Holy Spirit to occupy His rightful place in our lives and churches will we be enabled to fulfill the purposes of God.

Manuals and Outline Studies
by Fuchsia Pickett

Acts

Amos

Child Study

Ephesians

Esther

Hebrews

Holy Anointing

Holy Spirit - vol. 1

Holy Spirit - vol. 2

Hosea

How to Search the Scriptures

James

Job

Leviticus

Luke

Mark

Matthew

Proverbs and Ecclesiastes

Psalms

Romans

Ruth

Scriptural Study of Five Senses

Scripture Numerics

Song of Solomon

The Anointing

The Names of God

The Good Shepherd

What God's Word Says About Hell

A catalog listing other available printed materials as well as audio tapes may also be requested. To order, write or call:

Dr. Fuchsia Pickett
394 Glory Road
Blountville, TN 37617
(800) 398-0351

The Next Move of God
by Fuchsia Pickett

For two days God took Fuchsia Pickett into the Spirit and gave her a vision of the things He was going to do in the last days. He spoke to her about the coming revival and about how He would prepare the church for His return. With prophetic revelation and sound scriptural teaching Dr. Pickett now reveals *The Next Move of God*.

Available at your local Christian bookstore or from:

Creation House
600 Rinehart Road
Lake Mary, FL 32746
1-800-283-8494